Renew by phone o
0845 0020 7?
www.bristol.gov.uk/
Bristol Librar

D0528027

PLEASE RETURN BOOK BY LAST DATE STAMPED

27. JUL 08.

05. AUG 08.

29. SEP 08

07 NOV 08.

28/11/08

20. MAR 09.

- 4 JUL 2014

BR100

BSAL

21055 Print Servicess

About the author

Michael Norton is the UK's leading writer on fundraising. He has created several highly successful socially progressive programmes, including the Directory of Social Change (DSC), the Centre for Innovation in Voluntary Action (CIVA), Youthbank, Changemakers and unLTD (the Foundation for Social Entrepreneurs). He is also a Trustee of The Global Ideas Bank. Michael has written *The Complete Fundraising Handbook*, and a series of practical workbooks for young activists. Described by the *Guardian* as 'a one-man "ideas factory"', his latest book, *365 Ways to Change the World*, was published in 2005 and 2006 in the UK, Australia, Canada, India, South Africa and the USA to great acclaim. In 1998, he was awarded the OBE for his services to charity.

Need to know?

Fundraising

Michael Norton

Collins

This book is dedicated to Luke Fitzherbert who did
so much to promote effective giving and fundraising

Published in association with:
Resource Alliance
56-64 Leonard Street, London, EC2A 4LT
www.resource-alliance.org
and
Directory of Social Change
24 Stephenson Way, London NW1 2DP
www.dsc.org.uk

First published in 2007 by Collins
an imprint of
HarperCollins Publishers
77–85 Fulham Palace Road
London W6 8JB

www.collins.co.uk

A catalogue record for this book is available from
the British Library

Text: Michael Norton
Editor: Grapevine Publishing Services
Typesetter: Judith Ash
Series design: Mark Thomson

ISBN 978-0-00-724665-6
Printed and bound by Printing Express Ltd,
Hong Kong

Contents

Introduction

This book covers every aspect of fundraising. It is aimed largely at people who are working at a national, regional or local level raising money for smaller charities, and at community activists raising money for such things as their local school or hospital, local community and environmental improvement or any other sort of community initiative.

The first chapters explain the basic principles of fundraising and then go on to outline the different sources of support you might consider; these are then examined in greater detail. Many of the points are illustrated with simple case studies showing how things can actually be done.

The book as a whole covers the following main areas:

• Getting started – to give you the fundraising basics.

• What you will need to support your fundraising efforts – annual reports, leaflets, a website and publicity.

• How much you actually need – information about budgeting.

• Asking individuals – the many ways in which individuals can support you.

• Raising money through fundraising activities.

• Getting support in kind.

• Getting support from funding bodies: trusts, companies, government, Europe and the National Lottery.

• Putting it all together – adopting a fundraising strategy; using your time effectively; writing better applications.

• Sources of information and advice.

When you are fundraising you should always keep your goal in mind – with the money you raise, a need will be met, a problem solved or the wider world or your local community somehow improved. You will need to create a network of others who share your enthusiasm and who are prepared to help. That is the magic of fundraising – inspiring others to give, and using their support to change the world.

Just one final word of advice. There are lots of different ideas for raising money throughout this book, but you can't possibly attempt them all. Concentrate on just a few, and make them work really well. What you decide to do and how you do it, of course, are up to you, but remember that anyone can succeed in fundraising. All you need is to understand the basics and to have good information. The rest is just a case of a lot of effort applied in the right way.

So read the book, get started ... and the best of luck!

1 Understanding fundraising

There is a whole range of things that you need to do before you actually start asking for money. The first of these is understanding the fundraising process and the qualities you will need to make a success of it. How can you persuade donors to give money to you? What do you need to get started?

What is fundraising?

Fundraising means asking people to invest in your ideas and plans. You want them to share your concerns and your belief that something really does need to be done.

Must know

The deal

Fundraising is about selling people the idea that something can be done, and then creating a partnership in which they (the donor) provide the means and you (the activist) do all the work to make things happen.

Where do you start?

Fundraising is a mixture of your ideas, your past experience and achievements, your professionalism in planning and implementation, your determination, your enthusiasm and your communication skills (to convey all this). It is all of this that will determine your success.

As a starting point you will need:

• An organization or a group of people or an individual (you) who wants to address an issue, provide a service or create some sort of change.

• A project that you want to undertake, and your plans for doing so.

• The money to pay for the costs that you will incur.

• A fundraising plan for how you will raise that money.

• You, the fundraiser – you are the person responsible for raising the money.

But before we cover all of these, let's start with two important principles.

Principle 1: Fundraising is selling not telling
While you do have to tell people about what you have already achieved, about the problem you are addressing, about your plans and about the support you need, these are all the 'Whats?' of fundraising.

What you need to make sure they all know are the 'Whys?': why your organization has been successful; why your ideas and plans are terrific; why your project will make a difference; why it's a cost-effective use of their money; and most of all, why they should support you.

Principle 2: Fundraising is more than just asking for money

To be a successful fundraiser you must:
- Think before you ask.
- Know how to ask effectively.
- Proceed correctly once you have enlisted support.

Too many fundraisers write thousands of letters to people and organizations they hardly know (and who know little or nothing about them). It is important to think carefully about who might be interested in supporting you. Do some background research, and spend time developing and nurturing contacts so that you can get people enthusiastic about what you are doing and confident in your ability to achieve it.

The personal qualities you need

The right attitude is a good starting point. You need to be committed to the cause, and positive and enthusiastic about what you are raising money for. Next, you must learn to enjoy the challenge of asking for money. This usually develops quite quickly once you start to achieve some success.

It is often said of fundraising that it is not *what you know*, but *who you know*. But in actual fact, it is much more about *who you are*. Your personal skills in dealing with people, enthusing and persuading them

Must know

**Here are some of
the skills you need:**

The Ps
Passion
Persistence
Persuasiveness
Personality

The Cs
Commitment
Cheerfulness
Confidence
Creativity

The Os
Opportunism
Openness
Optimism

**Now think of some
more!**

to give are by far the most important attributes of a successful fundraiser and knowing your own strengths and weaknesses is vital.

Consider the following:
• What skills do you already have that will make you a successful fundraiser? If you are terrific on the telephone then this is a good vehicle for you to use for, say, asking for gifts in kind. You might be great at organizing events, in which case you can put together a dinner or sponsored walk.
• What skills can you develop and improve over time? You may have had limited success in certain areas but simply need more experience to really hone this.
• What are you absolutely hopeless at, and cannot see that you will ever be able to improve sufficiently? Do you shake with fear when called upon to speak in public or have difficulty in remembering people's names – if so, you must enlist the help of people whose strengths compensate for your weaknesses.

Two things that will help you enormously in improving your fundraising are:
• experience – i.e. learning from your mistakes, and
• success – as they say, success leads to success and even a small one will boost your confidence no end.

Persistence pays
To be a successful fundraiser you need persistence.

You've done all the hard work. You've identified a potential donor. You've done some background research. You've been in touch to find out whether they might be interested. You've written a proposal and sent it in. They've considered it. And then the answer comes back. And sadly, it's *'No'*.

Alex is the director of an arts centre. He loves to go to conferences. He studies the list of participants to see who he already knows, who has supported him and who he'd like to meet. In all the breaks he makes sure he talks to everybody. He's positive and enthusiastic. He hands out leaflets and visiting cards. He e-mails everyone afterwards with a bit more information about his organization and his plans.

Brian runs a community foundation, and needs the support of rich individuals and local companies. He has just given a rather flat presentation to about 25 people. A few questions were asked, and a couple of people expressed some sort of interest. Afterwards everyone had a drink, whilst Brian had a good gossip with his chums. Then everybody went home. And that was that.

Alex and Brian are different sorts of people. Which of them is the better fundraiser? Which is more like you?

Is this where the process ends? It shouldn't be. You marked them out as a potential donor. You put a lot of effort into approaching them. And this time, your proposal was rejected. If you don't try again you won't get anything; but if you do, there is always the possibility of a 'Yes'. Don't be embarrassed about going back. You have a number of options:
• Ask why they turned you down. Maybe they had just supported something similar? Or perhaps they had too many applications at that particular time? Your discussion could give you useful hints for the future. In any event, you will have developed a personal contact, which means that next time yours will not be just another application.
• Ask for an opportunity to explain your application more clearly to the people concerned. They may not

Think about this

• What fundraising skills do you have?
• What can you do to become a better fundraiser?

Must know

Perseverance

Many more requests are turned down than are funded. The likelihood is that you will get many more rejections than successes. Don't give up – which is what most people do. Go back with another request. Give them the feeling that you're not going to give up. Do everything you can to get their support.

have fully understood it and would possibly reconsider if they did.

• Ask them about their preferences. Perhaps they don't like paying for new equipment, but would support the running costs of your after-school club.

• Invite them to visit you to see your work at first hand and meet the people you are working with. This may inspire them to feel differently.

Coping with rejection

One of the biggest dangers that you face as a fundraiser is losing hope when people turn you down. But being turned down is a fact of fundraising life. So you need to learn how to deal with it.

Having your application rejected will inevitably make you feel miserable. You might believe that your project is no good, that you are a failure and then decide that you don't want to expose yourself to yet more humiliation by being turned down by the next person.

These are all very natural feelings. But it is all too easy just to give up. You might tell yourself, 'I'll leave it a few days'; 'I'll think of some easier way of raising the money'; 'I'll just send out letters – that way the rejection won't feel so bad.'

But you've got a fundraising plan and certain targets to meet. If you stop asking, you won't raise the money. There must be people out there who are interested in supporting what you are doing. Your job is to find them ... and to ask them as persuasively as you can to support you. Always approach those people who are most likely to support you first. Getting off to a good start will give you confidence!

Peter set a task for participants at his fundraising workshop, asking them to telephone every donor who turned them down and to try to get the decision reversed or lay the ground for a second approach. The results were really surprising. In around forty per cent of cases, participants were able to turn an original 'No' into an eventual 'Yes'.

Peter recounted this story at a conference on grant-making. The next speaker was the director of a large grant-making foundation. Anthea started by saying: 'Disregard what Peter has just said. When we say "No", we really do mean No.'

However, about six weeks later, Peter received a letter from Anthea. It contained a copy of a letter she had received from Helen at the Wirral Autistic Society, saying: 'Do you remember me? We met at the conference. You told me that a NO is a NO, and Peter said to turn a NO into a YES. I prefer to believe Peter, which is why I am writing to you again. You recently turned us down. These are the reasons why I feel that you should support us...' On a compliments slip attached to the letter, Anthea had written: 'How could I say "No" again? I sent them £1,500.'

Moral: too many people take NO for an answer. Be different. Pick yourself up, go back, try again. Try better. Give yourself a second chance.

What if?

In the event that your approach is rejected you must try to:

• Be thick-skinned – it is not you personally that is being turned down, even though it may feel like it.
• Take a rational approach – the more people you ask, the better your chances of success.
• Maintain your confidence and your enthusiasm – treat every approach as if it were the first; new contacts will not know about your previous attempts, so don't start by apologizing or being defensive.

• See failure as a challenge – think about why your application wasn't successful, try to analyse what happened and learn from the experience.

• Set yourself a target – decide in advance how many people you are going to approach each week and force yourself to keep to it regardless of results.

• Establish your own support group of people who you respect and who have experience of fundraising; their role is to tell you what a good job you are doing, that you are wonderful and how you might do better.

• Remember your goal – you are trying to raise money for something really important; if you don't succeed, people who are in need or the community as a whole will suffer. This should spur you on!

Jo wrote a book called *Colour in your Environment* for a national volunteering agency to encourage young people to become more active on environmental issues. She decided to try to sell it to bookshops.

She approached her local bookshop, and spoke to the manager, saying, 'I'm a local author and I've written this fantastic book. Would you like copies for your bookshop?' The manager replied, 'No. It's not the sort of book we're at all interested in.' Jo had a similar experience at three further bookshops. The excuses were different, but the result the same. She was ready to give up as it seemed so hopeless, but resolved to keep going. Again, she was rejected.

Finally she said to herself, 'Just once more, and then I'll give up.' She went to the Owl Bookshop in Kentish Town, London. The owner welcomed her with outstretched arms, said it was just the book they were looking for, bought 100 copies for the Christmas table, and asked what the next title in the series was going to be!

Moral: you might have to suffer many rejections along the way but somewhere out there are people who will be enthusiastic about what you are doing.

Taking and creating opportunities

The first thing to learn is to seize opportunities when they present themselves.

• A new grants scheme is announced: send off for information; be the first to apply.

• It is the International Year of the Older Person: you are raising money for a 'silver surfers' project; this is the year to do it.

• It is your fifth anniversary, or your founder has just been awarded an OBE: issue a press release; get featured in the local paper.

Make your own opportunities

Imagine you receive a letter with a small amount of money from a young person asking you to spend it for the benefit of less privileged children; she explains that this was her birthday money. You could either bank the money, and send off a nice letter of thanks for the very generous gift, or you might wonder whether if one young person has done this, there may be others who are willing to do the same thing, i.e. use this as a springboard for fundraising opportunities. In this case, you would contact the young person and ask if she would be interested in becoming a role model for encouraging other young people to give. You would then:

• Issue a press release launching a campaign for young people to give their pocket money to the appeal.

• Organize public meetings at which you and your very generous young donor speak about your work and plans.

• Develop a young members' scheme, and produce a leaflet publicizing this.

Get out and about

Fundraising is more than just sitting behind a computer screen, completing application forms and sending off letters and e-mails asking for money. You need to get out there.

Here are some things you might try:

Must know

Be active

Don't just sit behind your computer monitor. Get out and about! Spend at least ten per cent of your time (or even more) going to conferences, visiting projects, giving talks and meeting people. Use the phone to make contact, rather than just sending e-mails or letters.

• Ask a question or make a point at conferences. Introduce yourself and your organization when you do this.

• Ask each person in your team to arrange to give ten talks during the year. Think who might be interested in hearing about your work.

• Organize an open day, and invite people to visit you or hold a public meeting to talk about what you are doing.

• Pick up the telephone rather than sending an e-mail or a letter. Calling people allows you to get into conversation. You never know where this might lead. Schedule an hour per week or per month in your diary just for telephoning people.

• Make a list of all the people you really want to meet then find a way of doing it. If you can't think of any better way, then try just calling them up out of the blue. You never know.

What if?

• The Managing Director of a successful company (whom you have never met, but whose photo you have seen in the newspaper) arrives at a reception you're attending.

• You find yourself sitting next to a well-known television presenter in the waiting room of a large media company.

• You are invited to a lunch at which you will be introduced to the newly appointed Editor of a leading newspaper.

Think about what you could do in each of these situations. Then when equivalent or similar situations arise in your working or social life, you'll know what to do.

How giving works

Always remember that *people give to people to help people* – there are three people involved.

1. The donor

This is the person you are asking. Try to understand the situation from their point of view. What do they think about the issue in question? Why do they feel it is important? Will they benefit if something is done? What will motivate them to give?

For example, if you are raising money for a walk-to-school initiative, while you may be passionate about global warming, local parents' primary interest may be in seeing that their children get to school safely and on time, that they are not penalized by parking wardens or confronted by angry residents whose driveways they are blocking. Global warming might be a concern for one or two local parents, but certainly not all of them.

If, on the other hand, people have had some personal experience or contact with the problem, this can be extremely powerful. For example, if a family member has died of cancer, they may feel motivated to give to a cancer appeal.

2. The fundraiser

This is you. People will respond to *your* passion and enthusiasm. Make your appeal as polite, professional and personal as possible.

3. The beneficiary

This is the person for whom the money is being raised. Try to show how your work – and the money you are asking for – will actually benefit them, what

Must know

Golden rules

- Understand the donor.
- Be passionate and enthusiastic about what you are raising money for.
- Be knowledgeable and professional in dealing with donors.
- Build a reputation for being an organization that gets things done. If people have already heard about you before you even approach them, this will help.
- Involve your beneficiaries in any way that you can.

changes it will make in their lives and how it will help to solve the problem. Making it a point of practice always to involve the beneficiaries in your fundraising as much as you can will pay dividends.

Here are some good ways to do this:

• Use case studies, real-life stories showing how you have changed the lives of people.

• Introduce beneficiaries to the donor by organizing meetings where beneficiaries talk about the problem (or the solution) from their own point of view. This can have an enormous impact – whether it is young offenders talking about why they offend or how they decided to go straight, or children enthusing about a literacy programme you have been piloting.

• Bring the donor to the beneficiary by organizing a field visit.

Six degrees of separation

The idea of the six degrees of separation* is that anyone anywhere on the planet can be connected to any other person through no more than five intermediaries. For example, you know someone, who knows someone, who knows someone (and three more links) who knows the Secretary General of the United Nations, Bill Gates or the Thai chicken farmer you wish to speak to.

You have many contacts, and they in turn have contacts. So by asking people, and by asking them either to ask other people or to introduce you to them, you will be able to reach out personally to an enormous number of people.

A useful first step is to ask your colleagues, your committee or your membership to make a list of names (and e-mail addresses) of anyone they know who might be interested in helping you in some way. If you want to meet the Managing

* Six degrees of separation was first proposed by Frigyes Karinthy, a Hungarian writer, in 1929 in a short story called 'Chains'.

Director of a big local company, then ask if anyone knows him or her, or if they know someone who does.

What will make donors want to support you?

People are most likely to give money to your chosen cause if one of the following applies.

• They really believe in it and want to do something to help; there *are* people out there who care – your job is to find them.

• You have been able to persuade them, and now they want to help.

• They have a personal connection with the problem; for example, their child has died of leukaemia, their teenage daughter has suffered from eating disorders, their university is raising money for a new laboratory.

• They can see that they might be affected at some time in the future; cancer, heart disease and age-related problems, for example, are issues of concern to most people.

• They will benefit in some way, as in a school improvement project, brightening up the community, neighbourhood watch, and so on.

• They will gain personal recognition.

• They want to create a memorial for someone.

• They are being asked by someone they know and trust – statistics show again and again that the single most important reason why people give is *that they are asked*.

• There is some sort of tax relief involved.

• Someone rich, powerful and well known has already given – a celebrity endorsement can really encourage others.

• They trust you to do a good job – they believe that you are able to solve the problem and that you can spend their money in a cost-effective way.

The reasons for giving will vary from one donor to the next; you must understand the person you are dealing with and find the right way to motivate them.

Think about this

- What turns you on? What causes are you personally interested in? What motivates you to give? Why do you support particular causes?
- How do other charities present themselves when they are trying to raise money? Look at organizations doing similar work to yours. What factors do they highlight? And why?
- What do other people think? Talk to friends, experts, people experiencing the problem, the public at large. Find out their viewpoint.

The starving baby syndrome

The Asian tsunami unleashed a worldwide frenzy of fundraising. It happened the day after Christmas, 2004 and devastated whole communities, killing over 250,000 people. Almost everybody wanted to do something to help.

A fundraiser for an international aid charity need only present a picture of a starving baby and, again, most people want to help. The cause is compelling; the need is evident and it appears that with your help, a child's life can be saved.

Somebody who is trying to raise money for support services for schizophrenics, for prison reform or for avant-garde art, on the other hand, will have a much harder time. Their cause is not nearly as affecting, and they might find themselves thinking, 'It would be so much easier if I was raising money to feed starving babies.'

You are stuck with your cause, so you really do have to believe in it if you are to convey a sense of importance and urgency to the people whose support you are seeking. Of course, in the scheme of things, disaster relief and feeding the starving is fundamentally much more important than most other causes. But when you are trying to convince people, you need to make them feel that your cause is *really, really important*. And if you can't do this, you may as well give up fundraising.

Supplying the facts

Know your facts. People will ask you about your project and your plans, and you will have to be able to provide them with answers. Here are some of the things you will need to know.

• The extent of the problem or need. You shouldn't just say that there is a 'desperate need' and that it is 'urgent that something be done' about it. You should try to quantify the need and show the consequences of doing nothing.

• How many people will benefit. This is important. But equally important is the cost. These two facts put together show the cost-effectiveness of what you are planning.

• What other people are doing. You need to know what success others are having and how your project is different. You can point out the successes of an existing approach. Or you can explain why you are adopting a different course of action.

Inputs, outputs, outcomes and impact

It is important to understand the following terms.

• **Inputs**: these are the resources needed to make something happen – the time, money, expertise, equipment and facilities.

• **Outputs**: what you make happen. In the case of an after-school programme for children to improve their literacy and numeracy, the outputs are the number of sessions you organize and the number of children who attend and complete the programme ('bums on seats'). You should mention your outputs in your proposal as these will demonstrate your success in doing what you have promised thus far.

• **Outcomes**: these are the immediate effects on the beneficiaries. Again, in the case of your after-school programme, this will include any increase in literacy and numeracy skills. You will need a simple method for measuring the outcomes and you might want to take advice to ensure that you

---

Did you know?

Kerry Packer

Australian media magnate Kerry Packer died in 2005 aged 68, reputedly worth £2.75 billion. In 1990, he had suffered a near-fatal heart attack, and was clinically dead for six minutes before being revived by paramedics. One of his charitable contributions was to provide portable defibrillators for every New South Wales ambulance.

Cost-effectiveness

People are entrusting you with their money and worry that it might not be used effectively. Tell them about the number of people who benefit (the outputs), how they benefit (the outcomes) and the longer-term change (impact). Try to show that you are using their money efficiently to create a lot of benefit in return for the resources spent.

are measuring the right thing. For a very complicated programme, you may want to use a professional evaluator.

• **Impact:** the longer-term change that takes place as a result of your project. For the after-school club, it could include increased school attendance and learning attainment or decreased anti-social behaviour. You could also track the children's progress over a longer period and see whether more young people are going into further and higher education or if there is a reduction in youth offending. Many people predict an impact for their work; fewer actually set out to measure it.

Giving the reasons

If you were selling a product, you would work out the key selling points to persuade people to buy your product; these are sometimes known as Unique Selling Propositions, or USPs. Different people will buy the product for different reasons and you need to appeal to each of their particular interests and concerns. The same principle applies to fundraising: you need to tell people why they should support you.

The USPs of a pack of detergent might be:
• It washes whiter.
• It's soft on the hands.
• It's square-deal value.
• It removes even the toughest stains.
• It will make you a better, more caring parent.

Who should support a mural-painting project? The community generally, including the local council and local businesses: it will brighten up the community, reduce graffiti and vandalism and create good local publicity.

Parents of the children who will participate: it will provide an enjoyable summer-holiday activity over a period of one week, and teach children creativity, artistic skills and teamwork. This may persuade parents to pay the participation fee or to volunteer or to help with the fundraising.

Local residents living nearby: it will remove an eyesore, and might even increase property values. Include this in your door-to-door fundraising appeal.

Use these reasons when applying for a grant. Prepare the arguments you will use and select those arguments most closely related to the interests of the person or people you are asking.

Constructing a good case

Sometimes just a few key factors can be reason enough for someone to support you. Take the example of the British Geriatric Society who, some years ago, were trying to get a grant from a leading medical foundation. Their first attempt (which took the form of a rather long-winded summary of their work and their future plans) failed. The second time, they simply made the following points:

• That the elderly population was increasing rapidly – the over-65s would double over X number of years, and the over-75s would triple; these figures were obtained from government population trends.

• That the elderly consume a far greater proportion of health resources per capita than other age groups; the figures for this were available from government health data.

• That by putting these two factors together, the NHS would be facing a crisis if nothing was done; there was a ticking time bomb.

• That the British Geriatric Society, which is the 'trade association' of all doctors specializing in providing health

Must know

Creative thinking

• Always highlight the innovation factor in your fundraising – donors respond to this.
• Think creatively – think 'outside the box'. Use the *Problem Solving Handbook* from the Global Ideas Bank (www.globalideasbank .org).
• Visit other projects, talk to people. Be on the lookout for inspiring ideas that you can use or adapt.

care to the elderly, had a unique expertise that could be used to develop low-cost and effective health solutions for the elderly.
• That 'investing' in the British Geriatric Society would be a really cost-effective way of addressing a major health problem.

The result? A large grant.

Can you construct an effective case for what you are planning?

Innovation and creativity

Voluntary action thrives on creativity:
• Be resourceful in addressing existing problems.
• Identify and respond to new problems as they emerge.
• Find creative ways of generating an income to keep you going.

The Muhammad Ali factor

Muhammad Ali is thought by some to have been the greatest boxer of all time. As a young man, he was fond of saying 'I am the greatest!' Do you have the Muhammad Ali factor? Are you the greatest?

Complete these sentences using phrases such as the greatest, the best, the most important, the most urgent, the most innovate or creative, the most special. Doing this will boost your confidence; it may also convey aspects of your work that will particularly appeal to donors.

1. Our organization is the most ....

2. The problem or need we are addressing is the most ....

3. Our ideas for solving the problem or meeting the need are the most ....

4. Our team of staff and volunteers that will enable us to do this is the most ....

Two examples

In 2001 Mohammad Mamdani, a seventeen-year-old Londoner, set up the Muslim Youth Helpline, to provide advice to young Muslims on practical issues such as student debt, on cultural issues such as arranged marriages, and on societal issues such as unemployment amongst young Muslims and Islamophobia. Because MYH was set up by a young person for young people and is run with the help of a team of young volunteers, it can stress in its fundraising that it is the first and the best service reaching out to young Muslims.

In 1998, Eric Samuel set up the Newham Food Access Partnership to bring affordable fresh foodstuffs to people living in Newham, a place he described as a 'food desert'. He started by buying vegetables at the wholesale market and selling them cheaply and has gone on to create food co-operatives and social enterprises that promote healthy eating. Eric's pioneering role in food access, both locally and nationally, is a key factor in helping him to raise money for his future plans.

Building credibility

You need to be able to demonstrate that your organization will do a good job. Here are some things you should do.

List your successes. What has your organization achieved over the past few years? This might be work that you have done, but it could also be an important publicity triumph or a major grant you've obtained.

As a simple exercise, list four of your recent successes:

1. ....

2. ....

3. ....

4. ....

Think about this

If you have an idea, why not take it forward? Become a 'social entrepreneur'. Create new solutions for problems. Why not apply to UnLtd (if you live in the UK) for an award to help you to develop your ideas for a better community and a better world. A first-level award can be up to £5,000 plus a package of support. Awards are made to individuals with ideas, and not to existing organizations. www.unltd.org.uk

Write up some case studies. These can be quite long or just a short cameo (perhaps 30-100 words) and names can be changed if necessary for reasons of confidentiality (for example if you are a telephone helpline for people in real distress or a rape crisis service). Case studies can be a really important aid to successful fundraising. Prepare a stack of them (see pages 37-9) and use them in presentations, proposals and publicity material.

Gather together information that will boost your credibility. A good way of doing this is to create a 'Credibility File' into which you put:

• Promotional literature – ensure that your leaflets and reports are positive and well-written (see pages 34-7).

• Letters of endorsement from experts and prominent people saying how valuable and important your work is; if people visit you, ask them to write down what they thought of your work and whether they mind you using what they have written for publicity (and if nobody is visiting you, think about who you could invite along).

• Case studies showing the successes of your organization (see above).

• Photographs to illustrate how your organization works, how it benefits people and how much it is achieving; there is a general rule in communication that one picture is worth a thousand words so make sure you have some good photographs and video clips for use in fundraising presentations.

• Facts and figures about the need you are addressing and its importance.

• Extracts from evaluation reports that confirm your effectiveness and cost-effectiveness.

• Letters from users and beneficiaries showing how much your work is valued.
• Press cuttings about your organization – you can quote from these, circulate copies of them, or use them in a collage of recent press coverage; make good publicity really work for you.

Setting up an organization

If you are planning more than a one-off fundraising initiative, you may want to set up an organization to receive and spend the money that you raise. Your organization will need:
• A constitution that sets out its purposes and the rules by which it will be run.
• A bank account – for this you will have to provide a copy of your constitution and a Committee Resolution authorizing the setting up of the account.
• Proper accounts showing all your income and expenditure.

The two main types of organization
• **An unincorporated body.** This could be a Trust, a Society or an Association. In legal terms, this is no more than a group of people acting together, where they are all collectively responsible for what they do. It is simple to set up and will usually be sufficient in cases where you are not entering into contracts that create potential liabilities (such as employing staff where you take on all employer responsibilities, or taking a lease on a building where you become responsible for repairs and for continuing to pay the rent).
• **An incorporated body**, where the organization itself, rather than the group of people, takes on the liabilities. The most common type of organization is a Company Limited by Guarantee. But other possible structures include a Community Interest Company or an Industrial and Provident Society.

Do this

• List four recent successes, however large or however small.
• Put together some case studies.
• Buy yourself a box file, mark it 'Credibility File' – your task now is to fill it.

Case study

Leila went as a 20-something year old Voluntary Service Overseas volunteer to work with the Kenya Society for the Mentally Handicapped. They were starting from scratch, and her job was to help them get started in fundraising

Leila's first idea was to write to 100 local companies. She sent out a simple two-page letter, as there wasn't any money to produce a leaflet. The paper and printing were donated by a sympathetic printer. The letter raised a total of £850 from 22 companies.

In addition to the cash, the transport company TNT sponsored a medical camp, which their staff helped to organize, and they got their customers to donate medical help, medicines and clothes. Chandaria Bros, a hardware shop, provided lots of paint at cost for refurbishing special schools. Creative Business redesigned KSMH's logo and designed a poster campaign.

Rotary Clubs, Lions International, Inner Wheels and Women's Leagues meet regularly and often invite someone from a charity to come along as a speaker, so the next thing that Leila did was to telephone some of their local branches. She offered to speak about the KSMH Water Hyacinth Project, which makes paper products using water hyacinth fibre. As a result, she was invited to give several talks.

'Many Rotaries have their own agendas and are not always willing to support what you are doing. Don't give up; find the ones that would like to help you. Typically from each talk I would get ten people interested in helping. You need to ask for something specific, and you need to be persistent if you are to get anything to happen. The largest support came from the East African Women's League, who raised £1,300 for us through a school sponsored walk, a coffee morning and other activities.'

A printer that Leila met at one of these talks agreed to print 5,000 envelopes free of charge, which were used to collect donations. These were given to Safari companies to give out to tourists and to leave on tables in expatriate bars for customers to leave a donation. This effort only raised £60. If something isn't working, then think whether it is possible to do it better or differently – Leila decided to investigate the possibility of collecting money from air passengers.

All in all, Leila's first attempt at fundraising was a huge success.

You can get advice from:
- A Head Office body (such as the Scout Association for a local scout group), which will have a model constitution for member groups to use.
- An umbrella body such as Community Matters, which provides a model constitution and advice on setting up a community organization as a package deal costing £1,000 (see box right).
- A lawyer whom you instruct (for a fee or pro bono) to draw up your constitution; try to use a specialist charity lawyer for this (if you have to pay, it can cost £1,500 upwards).

Or you could adapt the constitution of an organization similar to yours. There will be some small out-of-pocket costs involved in this but doing it yourself will be almost free.

The Trustees

The Trustees are the people responsible for running the organization. They may also be known as the Directors (for a charitable company) or the Management Committee (for an association). They may appoint staff to actually do the work, or the whole thing may be volunteer-run. Either way, the Trustees are responsible for:
- Seeing that the organization operates within its objectives.
- Developing some sort of strategic direction for the organization.
- Ensuring that funds raised for a particular purpose are spent only for that purpose.
- Ensuring that the organization has sufficient funds to carry out its plans.
- Ensuring that proper accounts are kept.

Want to know more?

Useful (and free) sources of advice are:
- **Ask NCVO, a service from the National Council for Voluntary Organizations** with lots of free guidance on regulatory and governance matters: www.ncvo-vol.org.uk /asp/search/main.aspx
- The Charity Commission, which has a range of downloadable publications and model constitutions (see 'Registering a Charity' and 'Guidance for Charities'): www.char ity-commission.gov.uk
- Community Matters provides advice for organizations that are smaller and more local than NCVO members: www.community matters.org.uk
- See pages 75–9 for advice on Gift Aid, which can substantially increase the value of your donations.

2 Supporting your fundraising efforts

Literature, websites, newsletters, annual reports – the more documentation you can provide to demonstrate that you are a legitimate, worthwhile charity, the more people will be inclined to support you. It has to look professional, though, and be written in a simple way that grabs readers' attention.

What you will need

All you need to get started is a desktop computer and printer, along with a simple word processing package. With these you can produce a wide range of types of literature and you could even construct your own website. This chapter has some advice on how to do it yourself.

Do this

Think creatively about all the different ways in which you might get your leaflets circulated. Make a plan for distributing 5,000 copies.

Leaflets to promote your work

A well-produced leaflet explaining your work and encouraging support is extremely important. It should include a 'call to action' – asking people to do something specific – and a reply address and telephone number for further information. You may also want to produce fact sheets and case studies (see pages 37–9) offering more information to those who are interested.

Producing a leaflet is one part of the process – getting it circulated is the other. To get the leaflets out there, you could:

• Send a copy to everyone on your mailing list.
• Give copies to committee members, staff and volunteers to hand out to people they see at meetings and anyone else they come across who seems interested.
• Have copies in your office to give out to visitors.
• Send copies to potential donors with a short letter introducing yourself and your organization; this will lay the ground for an application at a later stage.
• Include a copy with all letters or packages you send out from your office.
• Ask your local newsagent to circulate your leaflet with newspaper deliveries.
• Post leaflets through all the letterboxes in your neighbourhood and beyond.

Producing a successful leaflet

A four-page A5 leaflet is a cheap and effective format. It could be printed in full colour, in black and one other colour, or in just a single colour. Here is a suggested structure for a simple leaflet:

Page 1: your name, logo and a strapline (a brief statement explaining the essence of your work).
A headline with a photograph and about thirty words of explanation.

Page 2: a brief history of the organization (in about eighty words, with a headline).
A table showing four key achievements.
A quotation from someone important.
A photograph of the organization at work with a caption (of about six words).

Page 3: a case study (in about fifty words, with a headline).
An explanation of the need with facts and figures or a chart (about eighty words, with a headline).
A photograph illustrating the case study with a caption (of about six words).

Page 4: your plans for the future (in about sixty words, with a headline).
A call to action: how you can help (about fifty words with a headline).
A reply coupon with tick boxes and room for the respondent to include their name/address/phone number/e-mail address.
A reply address with your telephone number for further information.
The leaflet should have a clear structure that takes the reader through from start to finish.

Producing an annual report

Donors will often ask for a copy of your latest annual report and accounts before deciding to support you. Many will also insist on seeing a copy for each year that they continue to support

Must know

Things to avoid in your leaflet

• **Don't be boring. You want people to pick up your leaflet and read it.**
• **Don't include loads of unnecessary information, such as the objectives of your organization as set out in your constitution, or lists of supporters, or a pompous message from your Chairman.**
• **Don't use vague generalizations. Give your readers hard facts and real examples.**
• **Don't produce a leaflet that is poorly designed and badly printed. This will suggest incompetence.**
• **Don't print your leaflet on expensive paper or thick card. This will suggest that you waste your resources.**

you. So it is clearly important to produce an impressive-looking annual report ... but what information should be in it?

• Organization details: name, address, charity registration details; the aims of the organization; a list of trustees (possibly with brief background information) and names of key staff and volunteers (with job titles and responsibilities).
• A brief history of the organization: why it was founded and its values; how it has developed.
• Your organization's main achievements. A useful exercise is to think of four achievements during the past year and four since the organization was founded.
• The problem or need that is being addressed and why it is important. Use census data, research reports and policy documents produced by government, think tanks and other agencies to illustrate this.
• Your working methods, and why/how they are effective or innovative.
• Case studies of people helped, with photographs if possible. These need not be lengthy, although you may want to write up one or two in greater depth.
• Endorsements and quotations that enhance your credibility.
• Where your resources have come from and how they have been spent. You could illustrate this in the form of a simple pie chart. You might also want to show how the organization has been growing over recent years, which can be illustrated by the growth in annual expenditure or the numbers of people you have helped.
• Your plans for the future.

• How people can get involved. Use every opportunity to tell people how they can help you – by giving money, volunteering their time or taking action.
• An address to write to for further information.

Designing your annual report

Your annual report should not only say what it needs to, but should read well and look good. While large organizations might have an in-house editor and employ a professional designer, smaller organizations probably can't afford to do this. Try to find people who can help you, such as:
• A journalist or someone in publishing who can assist with editing, either by giving you advice or by doing the work themselves as a volunteer.
• A graphic designer, who can either develop a simple format for you to use, or do the work themselves as a volunteer.

If you can't find anyone to help you, then the next best thing would be to find an annual report that you really like and use it as a model for your own. Print as many copies as you think you will need, plus a few extra for your archives.

Using case studies to tell stories

A case study can be used to show how the issue affects one person (the problem), or how you have been able to deal with that issue (the solution).

For example, if you are dealing with homelessness, don't just talk about why people in general become homeless. Instead, show how one particular person became homeless. Similarly, don't just talk about the services you provide, but show

Do this

Think about all the ways in which you might distribute your annual report. Work out a realistic print quantity. Circulate your report to donors, potential donors and other stakeholders.

how you have actually been able to help that person to get off the streets and into a more settled lifestyle.

Your case study could be based on a real-life example, or the names and details could be changed for confidentiality. Or, it might include features from several cases combined to create one 'composite' story.

Whatever angle you choose, case studies will focus your audience's attention on who you are helping, and will illustrate that their support will help real people. They will feel that their money can make a significant difference.

Example of a case study

Aruma is a widow living in the hills of Ethiopia. Life is hard. She has a small plot of land to grow food to feed herself and her three children, but the crops often fail.

When we began work in her village, Aruma was in debt, and her position seemed hopeless. She made a decision to borrow a small sum of money through our microcredit scheme so that she could purchase two goats. These provided her with milk, some of which she used to feed her family and some she sold. With this extra income, she started saving regularly. Quite soon, she repaid her original loan, and it wasn't long before she had saved enough to purchase an ox – which further increased her income.

Now Aruma is paying for her youngest child to continue in school, and she hopes that he will soon get a place at technical college and then go on to get a qualification in forest management. Like you and me, Aruma has her own dreams and ambitions. With your help, we can make her dreams come true – and we can also help others like her.

Some guidelines for writing case studies
- Explain the story in a conversational way and don't use jargon. Few people understand the word 'microcredit' (see the example opposite) or how it has the capacity to change people's lives.
- Excite people. Imagine that you are talking to someone at a party with real enthusiasm about the work you are doing – that's how you should be telling your story.
- Keep to the point. Between 50–200 words should be quite sufficient. The example opposite is 178 words.
- Give your case study a catchy headline. For the example opposite this might be, 'How to turn a goat into an ox ... and an ox into an education!'
- Include a good photograph.

Do this

Write a case study showing your impact on the life of an individual or a community. Find a suitable photograph to go with it. Keep a case studies file, so that you have a number of examples to hand when you need them, illustrating different aspects of your work.

Designing a great website

If someone wants to find out more about you, your ideas, your organization or the cause you are involved with, the first thing they will do is to type your name into Google. If the search comes up with nothing, then as far as the searcher is concerned you don't exist. So it is important that you get yourself a website. You can design your own, but if you don't know how to do this, you could:
- Find a professional website designer to do it all for you; the work might cost anything from a few hundred pounds upwards.
- Find a volunteer who would do it free of charge.
- Teach yourself how to do it; there are lots of how-to manuals around – just type 'Design your own website' into Google, and see what comes up.

What information should go on your website?
Many people just transfer the contents of their annual report to their website. This, however, can make for very boring reading.

Think about this

Your website should do the following:
• **Provide information on what you are doing.**
• **Create interest in your project.**
• **Encourage people to get involved.**
• **Provide a mechanism for people to give money.**

Try the following to keep it interesting:
• Edit the text, so that there are far fewer words, shorter paragraphs and lots of bullet points.
• Remove all jargon and acronyms.
• Use photographs and short case studies to bring things to life.
• Make it interactive – include a quiz so that people can test out what they know or a 'Did you know?' section with some startling facts.
• Provide links to useful related sources of information.
• Have a news section to keep people abreast of what's happening and to tell them about future events; make sure that you keep it up to date.

Once your website is up and running you need to think about ways of getting more people to visit it. Here are three suggestions for starters:
• Have a memorable website address, and use it in all your literature.
• Find ways of linking with other websites.
• Include a 'Tell a Friend' facility for people to send postcards.

Using your website for online giving

The easier it is for people to respond to your cause via your website, the more likely they are to do so. Here are some options for encouraging website visitors to give money:
• Include a donations form that can be printed out. This should include a postal address for people to return it to, together with their donation (cheque or money order). Make sure you include a Gift Aid declaration, so that you can reclaim the tax (see pages 75–9).

If you want people to give regularly, prepare a simple Standing Order form (see pages 78–9) for people to take to their bank authorizing a regular payment.

STAR

Student Action for Refugees (STAR) is not a big international organization; it is a student-led initiative on an issue that does not have wide appeal. But their website makes it easy for anyone to take action. It suggests that:

If you have ...

2 minutes ... click here and send an email postcard protesting against the trafficking in people.

5 minutes ... from pants to pop tunes, take this test www.refugee challenge.com and find out how much refugees have brought to the UK. Then forward the link to your friends!

15 minutes ... fax your MP protesting about the current asylum legislation. Find out who your MP is and their fax number here.

30 minutes ... design an awareness-raising poster and put it up at your school/college/university/youth club/workplace (being careful to get permission first if needed) to help spread the facts about refugees and asylum seekers.

a few hours ... look through your local/national newspaper and find any articles about refugees or asylum seekers. Look at the language they use. Is it fair/non-prejudiced? Write to the editor or letters page and make your views known. Send STAR a copy of the letter and let us know if you get published.

a regular time commitment ... find out where your local STAR group is or contact a local refugee project and see if they need volunteer support.

extra cash ... donate to STAR! Help us empower more students and young people to support refugees and asylum seekers everywhere. Please make cheques payable to STAR and send to: STAR, 3 Bondway, Vauxhall, London SW8 1SJ. If you would like to donate regularly then please contact us.

Take action on the refugee issue at: www.star-network.org.uk.

If you want to get membership subscriptions paid and plan to increase these from time to time, you will need Direct Debit. This is not easy for a small organization to set up – although the Charities Aid Foundation does provide a Direct Debit service at a price.

Do this

Use your website to encourage action. Make a list of all the things that people could do to help then put a selection of these on a 'Take Action' section of your site.

• Set up a 'Donations Hotline' – a telephone number that people can call to pledge or give money. When you answer the phone, you will take down all their details and the amount they wish to give. If you are registered to receive credit card payments, then all they need do is give you their name, their credit card details, their billing address and the amount they wish to give. You then process the transaction.

Ensure that the line is always manned when people call, or that there is an answerphone facility. If you are organizing a major appeal and are expecting lots of calls (say as a result of a TV programme), then contact Broadcast Support Services for advice: www.bss.org.

• Include an online donation facility on your website. There are a number of tailor-made services you can use, which are easy to set up, such as Just Giving, PayPal and WorldPay (see below).

Once you have an online donation facility up and running, you can signpost people to it in your promotional literature and publicity work.

Online donation

Just Giving is a commercial service for charities that provides an online donation facility whereby they collect the money for you and handle all the Gift Aid administration. You are charged a monthly charge (£15 plus VAT) and a percentage (currently five per cent) of the donations you receive is deducted to cover their administration costs. If most of the donations attract Gift Aid, then this adds twenty-eight per cent to the value of the donation – which more than covers the administration costs. Find out more from www.justgiving.com.

PayPal is an easy-to-use eBay service and is particularly useful for smaller organizations. It allows payments by credit or debit card (including payments from overseas supporters) to be received by you, without the bother of you having to set up your own credit card payment system. The transaction fees are 3.4 per cent plus £0.20 per transaction (with reduced rates if your turnover is £1,500 per month or more). There are no set-up fees or monthly charges. You can use PayPal for selling books, T-shirts, Christmas cards and other products from your website, as well as for donations. You will have to get the Gift Aid declarations and administer the tax reclaims but this is not difficult.

WorldPay is a similar service operated by the Royal Bank of Scotland, more suited to slightly larger organizations. Find out more from www.paypal .com/uk and www.worldpay.co.uk.

Do this

Invite visitors to your website to become members or friends of your organization, to donate money to you, or to purchase items from your website. Then provide them with the means to give you money.

Databases and record-keeping

It is important to keep good records of the people who have given to you. These include: big givers, regular givers and members, one-off givers and people who have shown an interest but not yet given. Your aim is to persuade people to move up the list, i.e. those who have shown an interest to start giving; those who have given to commit themselves to giving regularly; those who give regularly to think about giving more; those who give very generously to think about leaving a legacy.

To manage this process you need the following information about the people concerned:
• Name.
• Address.
• E-mail address.
• Telephone number (if they wish to let you have it).
• The category of giver into which they fall.
  In addition you need to know:
• How much they have given to you in the recent past.
• The date of their last donation.

Must know

Software

You can purchase proprietary software (such as DonorBase) to keep your records; or you can develop your own system using either FileMaker or Excel software. For a small organization with just a few supporters, Microsoft Word or even a manual system should be sufficient.

• When their current membership or standing order ends.

With this sort of information, you will be able to:

• Keep in regular touch with them via your newsletters and an annual report.

• Write to them asking for more support.

• Remind them to renew their membership.

• Invite them to attend events (talks, visits, celebrations, fundraising events, demonstrations, and so forth).

Always ensure your records are up to date. If someone has moved, their personal details change, or if an e-mail bounces back, amend your records immediately. You might also send a postcard from time to time asking people if their details have changed or if they no longer want to receive information from you.

You also need to prune your records if people are not responding. This is a matter of cost (the mailing out costs of sending them information) versus opportunity (the possibility that they might give at some time in the future). You could make a rule that if somebody has not given for two or three years, you will delete them from your database.

Understanding your supporters

It is really helpful to know who your supporters are and what motivates them to support you. Knowing this allows you to communicate with them more effectively and will give you a better idea of where to target your fundraising effort.

Send a questionnaire to everyone on your mailing list either by post or by e-mail (or both) with a covering letter, explaining why you are

Data protection

The UK Data Protection Act 1998 regulates the keeping and using of data about individuals in order to protect their privacy. The following are the eight principles of data protection. Personal information should be:

1. Fairly and lawfully processed.
2. Processed for specified purposes.
3. Adequate, relevant and not excessive.
4. Accurate, and where necessary kept up to date.
5. Not kept for longer than is necessary.
6. Processed in line with the rights of the individual.
7. Kept secure.
8. Not transferred to countries outside the European Economic Area unless there is adequate protection of information.

If you are a non-profit association or a smaller charity and are keeping personal data only for the purposes of maintaining membership or support for yourselves or for providing or administering activities for individuals who are either members of your organization or have regular contact with it, then you are exempt from registration under the Data Protection Act. Personal data should not be kept after the relationship between you and the data subject ends, unless and for so long as it is necessary to do so for the exempt purpose.

If you believe that you are not exempt, then you can get information on the requirements for registration from the Information Commissioner: www.informationcommissioner.gov.uk.

interested in their views. Give a closing date by which you would like a reply (around a couple of weeks – no more as if they don't reply quite quickly, they probably won't reply at all) and include a return envelope with a first class stamp (this will convey that it is important). You might even enter each reply into a draw as an incentive, whereby the winning reply receives a prize

Do this

- **Work out how you are going to keep your donor records.**
- **Set up a system for communicating with your donors.**
- **Keep your donor list up to date. Update records as people give you new contact details. Remove people who have not been responding for some time or where letters are returned.**

(donated of course!). Your questionnaire should comprise three sections:

• Contact details and personal details. You can ask them for their name, address, phone and e-mail details (although sometimes, especially if the information being supplied is of a personal nature, the replies may need to be anonymous). You will also ask about their occupation, age, type of involvement with your organization (as donor, volunteer, member, recipient of newsletter, etc.) and length of involvement with your organization. Sometimes a questionnaire will ask what newspaper a person reads as an indirect attempt to categorize their social class.

• Closed questions. These give the recipient a number of options to choose from, usually with tick boxes. This supplies you with data in a form that can be easily analysed.

• Open questions. These are answered by the respondent in their own words. The information is less easy to analyze, but very useful in that it reflects people's ideas about issues or solutions and can then be used as illustrative matter in a report.

Focus groups

An alternative to sending out a questionnaire is to conduct a group discussion, known in PR circles as a 'focus group'. This would enable you to explore issues in greater depth with existing supporters or with a random group of people who are willing to give up time to help you. If you organize a focus group it is worthwhile using a professional who is independent of your organization to conduct the session. This reduces the likelihood that your own strongly held views might affect the discussion. You might be surprised at what people come up with. Their perspective may be completely different from your own; their ideas and suggestions may be really creative.

The temperature of relationships

Successful fundraising is all about nurturing your relationships with people. The warmth of your relationships can be measured as follows:

Cold: the public at large who haven't supported you, haven't shown any interest in you (yet) and who may not even have heard about you.

Cool: people who may not yet have heard of you, but who might, in theory, have an interest in what you are doing – for example, bicycle riders for an organization addressing global warming, or families with teenage children for an eating disorders charity, or the local population for a local conservation society.

Warm: people who have shown some sort of interest in what you are doing – including past supporters, enquirers who have asked for more information about your work, visitors to your premises, participants in fundraising events, and friends and colleagues of trustees and staff.

Hot: your current supporters and volunteers – they are the people who have already made a commitment to help you.

The warmth of the relationship will determine how likely people are to respond and how generously.

Sample questionnaire

On the following pages there is a questionnaire for an environmental organization that wants to find out what its supporters think about global warming.

Think about this

Analyze your data with care. For example, if you find that most of your supporters are *Daily Telegraph* readers, this may be because the issue appeals particularly to middle-aged, right-of-centre, middle class people. On the other hand, it may be because this is the profile of the founding group who have since gone out and got all their friends to join. Or it may simply be that there was some good publicity for your organization in the *Daily Telegraph* once.

Questionnaire

We would like to ask you to take a few minutes of your time to help us. We are developing a strategy for addressing the issue of global warming, and we are asking you to provide us with some information on your attitudes to this issue. Could you reply by 23rd March. We enclose a stamped addressed envelope, so just complete the form and pop it in the post.

Everyone who completes the questionnaire will go into a prize draw, and the lucky winner will get a slap-up dinner for two at the delicious vegetarian restaurant, Manna from Heaven. Thank you in advance for helping us.

Contact details

Your name: ....

Your address: ....

Your telephone number (optional): ....

If they give you this information, it means that they are happy to be telephoned by you from time to time.

Your e-mail address: ....

This is important, as your e-mail address list must be comprehensive and up to date.

Personal details

Your occupation: ....

This could be an open or a closed question – see page 46.

Your age: ....

How you are involved with the organization?

❑ donor ❑ volunteer ❑ member

❑ newsletter subscriber ❑ other

Length of your involvement with the organization:

❑ 1 year or less ❑ 3 years or less ❑ more than 3 years

Which daily newspapers do you read? ....

Which other environmental organizations do you belong to?

....

You might also want to ask about their family status (whether they are single, live with a partner or live in shared accommodation and about the number of children who are living with them).

Travel by car

Do you drive a car? ☐ Yes ☐ No

What size is your car engine? ☐ 1,000cc or under
☐ 1,500cc or under ☐ 2,000cc or under
☐ over 2,000cc

Approximately how many miles do you drive each year?

....

What could you do to cut your annual car travel by half?

....

Journey to work

If you are in employment, how far is your workplace from your home
(in miles)?.....................................

Do you travel to work by:
☐ Car ☐ Car, sharing the journey with at least one other person
☐ Motorbike ☐ Public transport ☐ Bicycle
☐ Walk

If you travel to work by private transport, what is the main barrier to your using a more environmentally friendly form of transport?

Supermarket shopping

Do you buy your groceries and household goods at (tick all that apply):
☐ A supermarket ☐ An online store ☐ Local shops
☐ A farmer's market or box scheme ☐ Other

How far from your home is the supermarket you shop at?

....

How many times in a month do you shop at a supermarket (on average)?

....

Do you travel there by car? ☐ Yes ☐ No

What is the main factor preventing you from doing more of your shopping locally?.....................................

Travel by air
How many return trips did you make in the last 12 months?
Within the UK .... Within Europe .... Long haul ....
Would you be prepared to cut down your air travel by one half?
❑ Yes ❑ No
Would you be prepared to offset the CO_2 emissions of your air travel (which would mean making some financial contribution towards CO_2-reduction projects)?
❑ Yes ❑ No

You could also ask about such things as the journey to school, holidays, home insulation, green energy.

Your attitudes towards global warming
How do you rate global warming as an issue facing the planet?
❑ Extremely important ❑ Important ❑ Not particularly important
❑ Not at all
Do you feel that politicians are doing enough?:
❑ Yes ❑ No
What more would you like politicians to do?...............................
Do you feel that you yourself should be taking more of a stand on global warming?:.....................................
What is the one thing that you could do right away that would make an impact on your personal or family CO_2 emissions? ....

Thank you for completing this questionnaire.
Please return it to Mark Greenway, Newtown Environmental Campaign, 16 Green Street, Essex IG5 4LR or by e-mail to mark@nec.co.uk

Now it's your turn. Design a questionnaire that is easy to fill in and supplies the information you need.

Newsletters and e-newsletters

A regular newsletter (perhaps monthly or quarterly) is a good way to keep your supporters in touch with what you are doing. It gives you an opportunity to:

• Tell them about recent successes and achievements.
• Explain the issues and provide useful information.
• Keep them posted on upcoming events.
• Tell them how well you are spending their money.
• Ask them for more support (if you need it).

What makes a successful newsletter?

In order for your newsletter to be successful it should be:

• Interesting and inspiring; it should include viewpoints that may be personal or even controversial, not bland or boring.
• Well designed and printed, so that it looks good.
• Given a masthead or title design to create a sense of identity.
• Concise – make the contents short and sharp and give the articles eye-catching titles.
• Lively – create a personality for your newsletter.

Distributing your newsletter

Your newsletter should be distributed regularly and promptly. You can choose to:

• Post it or put it through people's doors (if you are a local organization and have volunteers prepared to do this).
• Send it by e-mail – this is immediate and cost-free, but not everyone has an e-address and it doesn't have quite the same impact as a printed newsletter.
• Put it on your website, where you can also archive all previous newsletters.

> **Must know**
>
> **Involve readers**
>
> Here are some ways of increasing reader involvement:
> • Allow space for readers' ideas and comments.
> • Make it a fun publication – you might include a quiz or a 'Did you know?' column or invite readers to find an answer to a problem.
> • Keep the content lively, interesting and informative.
> • Include some sort of 'call to action' in every issue.

Must know

Ways to improve your newsletter

• If it is being printed rather than photocopied, think about using two colours rather than just one. This adds to the cost, but does make the newsletter look much smarter.
• Ask a good designer either to design each issue or to provide you with a template.
• Keep it short – four pages of A4 is usually quite enough for a smaller organization; this can be printed on a sheet of A3 and folded.
• Show your efforts to a friendly journalist to check if you have got the tone and editing right.

• Take copies wherever you go to hand out to the people you meet.
• Target specific people whom you want to interest in your work (such as potential donors) and send them your newsletter with a covering letter saying, 'I thought you might be interested in what we are doing, and in particular in ...'.

Getting publicity

The more people who hear about what you are doing, the more likely you are to get support. So court publicity at every opportunity – in the local and national press, or on local radio or TV.
• Build good relationships with journalists – especially with the local media if your work is of mainly local interest. Telephone them from time to time to suggest an idea for a story.
• Issue a press release when something newsworthy is about to happen or has just happened. This could be the launch of an appeal, a significant achievement, an upcoming event, or the announcement of a substantial grant.
• Create photo opportunities. This might be a stunt or something involving a celebrity.
• Write a letter to the editor to air a good idea.
• Call a phone-in programme to give your point of view, again making sure that you mention your organization and its work.

Don't be embarrassed about being a publicity-seeker; you need to draw attention to the issue, get publicity for your work and to build your organization's reputation. Start by devoting five per cent of your time to publicity – that's a couple of hours a week. Some of your attempts at getting media coverage will go nowhere but don't be disheartened. You will eventually succeed.

How to write a press release

A good press release comprises the following:

- A catchy title that explains what it is about and draws the reader in.
- A first paragraph that explains clearly why it is newsworthy and important.
- Subsequent paragraphs that tackle 'the Five Ws':

What: what has happened/is about to happen;

Who: who is involved (the press really like celebrity involvement);

When: when it happened/will happen;

Where: where it happened/is going to happen;

Why: why it is important and newsworthy; tell them, don't leave it to them to work out.

- Short sentences and lively language (avoid jargon).
- A quote from someone important (your Chairperson, Chief Executive, an expert or a celebrity); if you put this in inverted commas, it can then be used to give the impression that the publication interviewed the person themselves.
- A contact name and phone number; ensure that person will be available and can be trusted to handle queries or give interviews.

In addition:

- Use one-and-a-half-line spacing for readability, and staple the pages together.
- Do not exceed two pages – that's quite long enough.
- Always date your press release.

Do this

Keep a list of names and addresses of journalists working on newspapers, magazines, journals, radio and TV who might be interested in covering your work and send them a press release when something newsworthy happens or is about to happen. If you think that a specific journalist might be particularly interested, telephone them just after you have sent out your press release.

Think about this

- **Don't print more copies than you need; it's expensive and a waste of paper. But do think creatively about how you can circulate more copies.**
- **It's better to produce a really good newsletter less frequently than to send out something mediocre more frequently – less is more!**
- **Why not distribute your newsletter by e-mail, if you can get people's e-addresses? Distributing your newsletter by e-mail can have several advantages. It will: save you the cost of printing and postage; enable you to include links to other websites and to video and audio clips; allow you to send out a special edition quickly if there is something urgent to communicate.**

• Only send supporting material if it is relevant and do not staple this to your press release.

Once you have written your press release, read through it. Edit it ruthlessly and if in doubt, leave it out!

Volunteers and local support groups

You will need lots of volunteers for your fundraising; the more you have, the more money you are likely to raise. Your volunteers can get involved in many areas of your work including:

• House-to-house and street collections.
• Helping out at a fundraising event – at the desk for registration, as marshals on a sponsored walk, general troubleshooting.
• Soliciting gifts in kind, brochure advertising or subscription renewals – volunteers with a good telephone manner might be just what you need.
• Selling raffle tickets or Christmas cards.
• Speaking at meetings – you could recruit a small team of volunteers to speak at schools, Rotary Club lunches or for anyone who is interested in knowing more about your cause.

It is important to manage your volunteers effectively. This means ensuring that they understand your organization's work and aims and maybe them even meeting and talking to some of the beneficiaries, where possible. If they are likely to be with you for some time it may be worthwhile investing in a training course; otherwise you can train them yourself.

Give your volunteers a clear job description, so that they know what is expected of them. You should agree challenging but achievable targets with them and do all you can to maintain their enthusiasm and commitment. Recognition of their efforts and thanks are extremely important in this respect.

Starting a local group

Someone who lives in the next town has approached you wanting to help. They are committed, enthusiastic, energetic and well organized. You suggest to them that they might form a local group to raise money with you, to which they agree. What do you do next?

• Go through your supporter records to find anyone in their town who has expressed an interest.
• Suggest that they ask friends and colleagues if they know people who might be interested.
• Try to get a letter or a short article in the local paper asking for people to contact you.
• Push leaflets through people's doors.

Anyone who is interested is then invited to tea or for a drink to hear about the organization and its work and about your plans to recruit a group of local volunteers to help.

Even if only a few turn up, that's a start; try to get them to agree to do something as soon as possible. As the group develops and begins to raise real money, it may be worth thinking about setting up a second group, then a third …

Want to know more?

• See chapter 8 for more tips on writing concise, effective copy for your leaflets, newsletters and website.
• *The Writers' and Artists' Yearbook*, published annually by A & C Black, lists national newspapers and magazines to which you might want to send press releases.
• You'll find local papers listed in your local phone directory.
• There's information on organizations that may be helpful to you on pages 188-9.

3 How much do you actually need?

Putting a price on your goals can seem like asking how long is a piece of string, but it should be the starting point for any fundraising campaign.

Calculations and costings

In order to calculate how much you will need, you have to break down your costs, including overheads, into simple categories that you can put an accurate price tag on.

Analyzing costs and preparing budgets

Before you get down to preparing a budget, think about how you plan to spend the money raised. Will the money be used:

• For the organization as a whole, to go into general funds and be spent as you decide?
• For a specific project or activity, in which case you tell people how you will use their money?
• To cover the costs of providing for a stated number of beneficiaries – for example, to sponsor one child or pay for ten eye operations; the donor's support is then matched to particular areas of work?
• To pay for a specific item of expenditure, such as a new computer or repairs to the roof or one staff member's salary?
• To go towards a capital appeal for a new building ?
• To build a reserve fund to help secure the organization's future?

Raising money for a specific project or activity will always be far easier than raising it for your general running costs or to put into reserves, because it enables you to focus attention on the beneficiaries and the benefits of the work you are planning.

Of course, you will be incurring all sorts of general running costs including: office expenses and stationery; keeping accounts and the annual audit; the costs of fundraising and getting publicity; organizing Trustee meetings.

To cover your costs you have two options:

• Obtain general funding or use your membership income (if you have members) for this.
• Allocate your general running costs to your projects, and include this in your project budget. When you raise money for your project, you will also be covering a share of the overheads. This is the basis on which accounts are normally prepared anyway.

Preparing a budget

There are several steps involved in preparing an effective budget.

Must know

Using professionals

If the finance of your project is complicated, ask around to find an accountant or book-keeper who might be prepared to volunteer their time to oversee the accounts for you.

Step 1: Define your project

Work out exactly what you plan to do in as much detail as you can. Think about all the activities you will be undertaking and the expenditure you will incur. Discuss your plans with the people who will actually be doing the work. It is important to get their input.

Step 2: Cost each item of expenditure

List each item of expenditure, then estimate the cost. This will call for some basic research – if your estimate is too low, you will not raise enough money, but if it is too high, you might look unprofessional. For substantial items, ask for quotes from several suppliers; for smaller items, a rough estimate is sufficient.

Step 3: Calculate the overheads

Allocate a fair share of organizational overheads and staff time to your project budget.

Step 4: Include a contingency sum

Things will not always work out quite as you expect. Sometimes you end up paying more – either because you have underestimated a cost, or because you overlooked it in your costing. A contingency sum will allow for this.

Do this

Put theory into practice: work out a budget for your next project.

Step 5: Review your first attempt at a budget

Add up all the costs and look at them in relation to the work you plan to undertake. Does the total seem to be in keeping with the outputs and outcomes you are promising? You will always find some areas where you can make economies.

Step 6: Finalize your budget

Discuss your draft budget with colleagues. If you are looking for a large grant, you might consider discussing the budget with the donor before submitting the proposal. Use this feedback to prepare a final budget.

Budget example 1

What you want to do: you are planning a sponsored walk to raise money for your project. It will be organized by a group of volunteers (so there will be no staff costs). Your task is to draw up a budget and as you have been doing this for a number of years your first step is to look at last year's plans, to see how much everything cost.

What you will spend the money on:
• Printed matter: leaflets describing the work of the organization, sponsorship forms, posters.
• Volunteer briefing: facilitation costs and hire of a room.
• Volunteer expenses: sundry out-of-pocket costs for the organizing team and for volunteers on the day.
• Promotional materials: t-shirts for officials, banners to use on the day.
• Refreshments for participants.
• Sundry: public liability insurance, general overheads, contingency.

How much you will be spending: work out an actual cost or a reasonable estimate of what you plan to spend on each item.

Leaflets: lots of these have already been printed at a cost of 12p each, so you will not need to print any more. You plan to use 1,200 copies, giving them to participants for the people they are asking to sponsor them. You also need to have copies available on the day. The cost to put in your budget is £144. This money will not actually be spent, but will go towards reprinting the leaflets when your present stock is used up.

Photocopying: you will photocopy promotional posters, sponsorship forms and instructions for participants. A local photocopy shop has offered you an all-in price of 3p per page. You estimate that you will need to print 1,500 pages. Allow £45.

Volunteer briefing: you are using a local community hall for the session, at a cost of £50. Hiring a facilitator, which you plan to do through a small consultants group that has been recommended to you, will cost you £100.

Organizing team expenses: the organizing team of six people will meet five times. You will cover their travel and babysitting costs as well as coffee and biscuits. Allow £20 per meeting, which seems reasonable. Total cost: £100.

Volunteer expenses: you will be paying expenses for volunteers on the day – twenty people in all (including the six members of your team). They will require travel costs, sandwiches and drinks. Allow £6 per person. Total cost: £120.

Promotional materials: a t-shirt company has quoted for twenty t-shirts and tabards at £12 each including design and VAT. Total £240. You already have banners you can use.

Refreshments for participants: you have agreed an overall sum of £70 to pay for bottled water, soft drinks, biscuits and the cost of transporting them from the supermarket.

Sundry: you have a quote for £50 for insurance to cover you against accidents.

The total costs so far are £919. In addition you should allow a contingency sum (ten per cent is reasonable), in this case £92. There is also the cost of keeping the organization going: membership of the local Council of Voluntary Organizations, holding your AGM and preparing your annual report and accounts are the main costs. These total £400 and your sponsored walk is one of three fundraising events you organize during the year. So add £150 as the contribution towards overheads, which is approximately one-third.

The budget for your event is as follows:

Printing and publicity	190
Organizing costs	250
Volunteer costs	270
T-shirts and banners	240
Refreshments	70
Sundries (insurance)	50
Contingency	92
Total:	**£1,162**

You have included the overheads with the organizing costs, and included banners with the t-shirts.

How you plan to raise the money: you are projecting that you will have seventy people participating, each pledging to raise at least £50. You estimate that you will raise at least £5,000. Last year you managed to raise £5,570. The costs look reasonable in relation to the projected income.

As far as the fundraising goes, you will try to get as much donated as possible. You will also ask the local estate agent to be the 'event sponsor' for a contribution of £500. You want as much money as possible to go to your work.

On the day: on the cost side, everything went as planned except you forgot that you needed signposts around the route of the walk – a member of the team constructed these for you, but required £12 for timber; you also forgot to ask the consultancy if their fee included VAT – this *was* payable on the £100 fee, which meant an extra £17.50; and you later decided to give a small 'prize' to all participants completing the course at a cost of £70. The extra costs came to just under £100, more or less covered by the contingency. On the income side, you managed to beat last year's total, and you did get a sponsor for the event plus the refreshments donated in kind.

Budget example 2
What you want to do: you are working for a local youth organization that is planning a ten-day summer holiday activity programme for fifty young people aged fourteen to sixteen in the neighbourhood. The theme of the programme is global warming and what people can do to make changes. It will include drama, creative arts, visits and discussions. The young people will work in small groups on a project. There will be a party at the end organized by participants.

What you will spend the money on:
• **Programme costs**: community centre hire, session costs of two tutors and facilitators (plus yourself), volunteer expenses – sundry out-of-pocket expenses for five speakers and six volunteers, materials and other project expenses.

• **Cost of the party.**
• **Promotional costs**: publicity costs to promote the event, invite people to apply and select the applicants (each of whom will be asked to contribute £10); you will also have a photographer coming on two days to photograph the event, which you will use for future publicity.
• **Sundry**: sundry costs include meeting child protection requirements, insurance, organizational overheads and a contingency.

How much you will be spending: work out an actual cost or a reasonable estimate of what you plan to spend for each item.

Programme costs: you have already made a booking for a community centre for the ten days and agreed a cost of £750. The Youth Service advises you that a reasonable session rate for tutors is £200 per day. So this will cost you £4,000. Volunteer expenses and tutors' out of pocket costs are estimated at £30 per day or £300 in total. You set a budget of £1,200 for all the other programme costs and £350 for the party. You've never done anything like this before, so you are not sure if it will be enough or too much. But you will try to stick within this budget.

Promotional costs: you need to prepare a simple leaflet; you will print some copies and send some out by e-mail. You estimate the cost at £200. The photographer is charging £300 for two half days.

Sundry: your organization already has an insurance policy to cover this project, and procedures and a policy for child protection are in place. But you reckon that the event will take two months of staff time to organize and deliver. The salary cost is £2,400 (including National Insurance), and you

add the same again to cover organizational overheads.
The total cost is £4,800.
Contingency: you decide to put in a nominal £300
as contingency.

The budget for your event is as follows:

Programme costs	1,850
Tutors and facilitators	5,200
Venue hire	750
Volunteer expenses	300
Organizing and preparation	2,900
Office and sundry	1,200

Total: **£12,200**

This all seems very reasonable. The cost works out at under
£250 per person. This budget shows half the staff time and
overheads allocated for facilitation, because one staff
member will be acting as a facilitator, partly for organizing and
preparation and one quarter as overheads. The contingency
is added to the programme costs. Volunteer costs are listed
separately. This is all done to make your budget appear more
attractive ... which makes the fundraising easier.

How you plan to raise the money: your costs and office
costs are actually paid for through your annual grant received
via the Youth Service. That amounts to £4,800. It is still
worth showing this as a cost, as it demonstrates the real cost
of the project and the contribution that your organization is
making to the total cost. In addition, you plan to put in an
application to the Awards for All scheme for £5,000, and
participants will contribute £500, leaving £1,900 still to be

raised. This is not a huge amount. You are considering two ideas for raising this: a fundraising scheme whereby each participant is asked to raise £25, and writing to a number of small local trust funds.

On the day: it actually all worked out pretty well.

The project fitted the guidelines of the Awards for All scheme; you put in your application in good time and it was successful. You developed a really interesting idea whereby participants surveyed twenty-five people on their carbon dioxide emissions, each of whom was asked to contribute £1 towards the cost of your project. This raised £880. You received two donations of £500 through your fundraising efforts, and were able to get quite a lot of the materials from a Children's Scrapstore. Your main problem was controlling the costs to ensure that they came in at or under budget.

Key budgeting issues

• Know the cost of everything. It is easy to budget for the money you spend on purchasing goods and services. But every project involves some overheads and (where staff are employed) staff time. Allow for these either by making an estimate of total costs and the percentage that should be applied to the project or by working out the amount of time (in days) needed and then doubling it to allow for overheads. If you don't do this, you will always be asking for too little.

• Some aspects of your work will be harder to fundraise for than others. In a hospital, for example, it is much easier to fund the children's ward than it is the old people's ward or the psychiatric unit. It may be possible to allocate general funds (such as membership income) towards those areas that are harder to raise money for.

Do this

Make your own list of people you want to involve and how they can help you.

• Fundraising and administration costs. Nobody likes paying for these, and people always try to calculate them as a percentage of your total costs in order to see how efficient you are. What is a reasonable administration cost depends on the nature of your project; but good administration is essential for a successful project. One thing you can do is to allocate the costs of administration and fundraising across all the project budget heads so that they become part of your project costs; another idea is to give them other names such as 'publicity' or 'education' or 'outreach'.

• Who sets your agenda? It is easy to fall into the trap of doing what your donors are prepared to pay for rather than doing what you want to do. You must develop your own priorities rather than have your parameters set by what your donors are interested in funding.

• Missing items. It is extremely easy to forget items of expenditure and leave them out of the budget. You could then draw up a revised budget and use this to raise more funds. Otherwise you will end up out of pocket. Use your past experience to ensure that you have considered everything.

• Seriously underestimating your costs. This is a frequent problem – partly because people are too optimistic, and partly because they are frightened of constructing a budget that seems too high. Do your very best to estimate all the larger items of cost accurately.

• Allowing for inflation. Some budgets are for more than one year; make a reasonable allowance for inflation for all years beyond the first.

• What happens next? Many donors want to know what you plan to do once the project has been completed. If you can

Do this

• **Put a reasonable value on the volunteer time and on the things that are donated. Use the minimum wage or an assessment of what the cost would have been had you paid for that time (which is likely to be higher).**
• **Gifts in kind: make a rough assessment of the value of what has been donated.**

show ways of generating some of the income you need to continue the project or of finding it from another source, your project will be more attractive to donors.

Goonj

Goonj is an award-winning organization based in Delhi. It recycles clothing and other unwanted goods aiming to get them to those who need them – to the poor and for disaster relief. They collect clothes, toys, utensils, blankets, medicines, stationery, old newspapers, magazines and used paper. Teams of volunteers sort the donated items and send them to where they are needed.

This is what Goonj asks different groups of people or individuals to do:

• Organizations or companies: to motivate colleagues to volunteer; initiate a collection drive; donate unwanted paper, equipment and furniture.

• Potential donors or sponsors: to support Goonj's camps, events, products and administrative expenditure.

• Manufacturers: to donate surplus materials and items that can't be sold (such as cloth, garments, footwear, stationery, toys, books, utensils, furniture etc.).

• Banks: to offer bank premises for collection of donated items and to display publicity material.

• Actors or theatre directors: to help with street-plays and to sensitize the public about Goonj's work.

• Shopkeepers: to use paper, cloth or jute bags made by Goonj instead of plastic bags.

• Airlines: to give free tickets to enable the organization's staff to travel across the country to meet beneficiaries, understand their needs and to widen the charity's network.

• Schools or colleges: to initiate a collection drive and discuss the issues of poverty and natural disasters.

• Anyone and everyone: to volunteer with Goonj, donate whatever they can and tell all their friends about the organization.

Accounting for volunteers and gifts in kind

You may think that if things are donated you need not include them in your budget. However, this is a mistake – always include the cost of volunteers and gifts in kind in your expenditure budget, and also the equivalent of donations of time or in kind in your income budget.

For example, a community in Africa is building a well with the help of an international aid agency. The agency is putting up £1,500 to pay for cement, equipment and the services of an engineer. The community is providing manpower and some of the materials.

Let's say that the community is contributing 1,000 hours of volunteer time (which we could value at the minimum wage of £1.20 per hour), and materials that would otherwise cost £300 to purchase. A budget could then be constructed showing the community contributing £1,500 to a total budget of £3,000:

Income		Expenditure	
Grants	£1,500	Engineer	£850
Value of donated materials	£300	Labour	£1,200
Volunteer time	£1,200	Cement	£500
Other materials	£300	Equipment	£150
Total income:	**£3,300**	**Total expenditure: £2,700**	

Presenting the budget in this way shows the real cost of the project. But it also illustrates that the venture is a partnership between the agency and the community, which donors will find attractive.

Want to know more?

• Buy an accounting package such as Excel to help keep financial records.
• See pages 75_9 for advice on Gift Aid.
• Chapter 7 explains how to contact government bodies and charitable trusts who might be willing to give a grant to your organization.
• There are useful organizations listed on pages 188-9.

4 Raising money by asking individuals

Nobody wants to waste time approaching people who are unlikely to give money or on organizing activities that don't deliver. This chapter looks at ways you can approach individuals for one-off donations, regular contributions and legacies.

Finding people who will help

Individuals contribute around thirty-five per cent of all the money that is raised for charity in the UK. They are an important source of support for any organization. What you need to do is find those people who might be interested in supporting you and persuade them to do so.

Think about this

While one-off small donations are important, the real benefits come when you can persuade your donors to commit to giving regularly, to increase the amount they are giving, to consider donating a major gift and, ultimately, to leave your charity a legacy in their will. As a fundraiser, you must persuade as many of your supporters as you can to increase their level of commitment.

Who gives to charity?

In 2003–04, the charity income of the UK voluntary and community sector was £26.3 billion. Of this:
• Thirty-eight per cent came from the public sector.
• Thirty-five per cent was voluntary income given by individuals.
• Fifteen per cent was internally generated (from charges and investment income).
• Ten per cent came from charitable funds (trusts and foundations).
• One per cent came from the private sector (company support is not huge).

What sorts of people give?

Your potential donors include men and women, young people and older people and everyone in between. In fact, anybody and everybody, but especially:
• Family, friends and work colleagues of your staff, your committee, your volunteers, your existing supporters; the personal connection makes it easier for you to approach them.
• Local people – for a neighbourhood cause, you should look for support from all local residents.
• People who are/have been affected by the problem or are in some way involved with it are also likely

supporters (e.g. families of hospital patients for a hospital appeal, parents for a school appeal, etc.).
• People with a known interest in the issue – Friends of the Earth supporters, for example, might be particularly interested in a local environmental campaign, or library users in a literacy campaign.
• Professionals such as lawyers or doctors or scientists or teachers, where there may be a connection between their professional interest and what you are doing.
• Members of a social organization, such as a campaign, Rotary Club or professional association, political party or trade union, and faith groups; you can ask to circulate information to their membership or be invited to speak at a meeting.
• Children or students, whether for educational reasons or because what you are doing interests them.

Why do people give?

If you understand *why* people donate money to charity, then it's easier to enlist their support. There are many reasons and motivating factors ranging from first-hand experience or connection with the cause to personal recognition and tax relief (see pages 75–6). You must identify who the right people are and how to appeal to them.
• Think about the sort of work you are doing and who is likely to be interested in supporting you.
• Look at who is already supporting you and try to find out why.
• Test different audiences to see their response to your cause; you will almost certainly find that what you are doing interests quite a wide range of people.

Types of donation and support

There are many ways in which people can choose to give money:

• One-off donations – because you have asked them or because they have heard about your work and want to help.

• Regular donations, whether monthly or quarterly or annually, paid by Standing Order or Direct Debit or by using a Payroll Giving scheme (see pages 79–80).

• Membership – by paying an annual subscription they may then feel that they 'belong' to the organization.

• A major gift towards an appeal or sponsorship of a project or programme.

• A legacy.

The Giving Pyramid

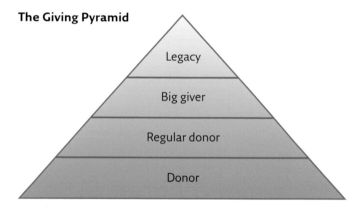

As you go up the pyramid, the donations become larger, but the number of people making them is smaller.

Other ways in which people can support you

If there are people who want to support your organization but not necessarily by donating money, they can:

• Join a supporters' group, which meets from time to time either to hear more about your work or to help with fundraising.

• Make a gift in kind – this might be anything from offering you office space to giving you items to sell at a charity auction.

• Volunteer specialist skills (such as legal or financial work/advice) or their time (stuffing envelopes, delivering newsletters, or whatever is needed).
• Raise money from their family, friends and colleagues at work.
• Make a loan or guarantee a bank loan to your organization; this could be useful when you are acquiring an asset.
• Give shares in a company – there is a special tax relief that makes this form of giving particularly attractive.
• Participate in fundraising events such as a dinner or a sponsored walk.
• Encourage their employer to support you – some big companies have matched giving schemes, whereby they match the time given by an employee or the amount the employee gives or raises.

Gift Aid for tax-free giving

While getting tax relief on a donation is never anyone's main reason for giving, it can be a strong incentive. There are two ways in which tax relief can be beneficial:

1. **The charity benefits**: in the United Kingdom, the tax relief on charitable giving is called Gift Aid. The charity receives the major part of the tax relief and charities are, therefore, usually very keen to take advantage of it. At the present tax rates (basic rate Income Tax is twenty-two per cent and Higher Rate Tax is forty per cent), a charity claiming Gift Aid relief will receive an extra £2.82 for every £10 donated (i.e. £12.82 in total) and a donor who pays Higher Rate tax will save £2.31 (so the donation will have cost them only £7.69).

2. **The donor benefits**: in the United States and in many other countries, it is the donor who gets all of the benefit. So if the tax rate is twenty per cent, the charity will receive the $10, but the donor will be entitled to claim $2 in tax relief.

Must know

Tax relief

Make sure that you understand tax relief and how you and your donors benefit so that you can use it whenever you are trying to raise money from individuals. It's really quite simple, and it will help you to generate even more money! For more information, go to the HM Revenue and Customs website www.hmrc.gov.uk/charities.

When is Gift Aid applicable?

Gift Aid tax relief is available only in certain circumstances.

• The donation must be made by a taxpayer: the donor should be paying UK Income Tax or Capital Gains Tax so that the tax paid is at least equal to the amount of tax being reclaimed on the donation.

• The donation must be to a registered charity; the donation should be made to an organization that has charitable status.

• You can only claim tax relief on the donations you make, not on money you collect; you're not supposed to claim tax relief on money you have collected from friends and colleagues, for example when you are doing a charity walk or running the London Marathon. It is the people who are supporting you who would need to sign a Gift Aid declaration on the amount that they are giving.

• The money should not be a payment for something that benefits you: tax relief is available only on donations, and not on payments for goods or services. It is possible for the charity to split a payment into two parts: a reasonable payment for tickets (say to a dinner) plus an optional donation on top of this amount.

• The necessary paperwork must be in order. The donor has to sign a Gift Aid Declaration. The charity has to provide some sort of evidence of having received the donation and can then claim the tax relief by filling in forms and sending them off to the Inland Revenue. The Inland Revenue occasionally pay visits to inspect a charity's books of account.

Note: Some donors may send you charity cheques or vouchers or a payment from a Charities Aid Foundation

*account. You can't claim Gift Aid on these as it has
already been claimed on behalf of the donor.*

Examples of how to collect Gift Aid
A sponsored walk
John is planning to run in the London Marathon to
raise money for the local hospice. He has pledges
from eighteen people totalling £385.

Janet, the hospice's fundraiser, explained to John
that if he successfully completed the marathon and
collected all the money pledged he could add a
further £108 to the amount he raised by persuading
his donors to sign Gift Aid declarations.

In the event, twelve of John's donors completed
the forms (for donations totalling £317), two forgot
to (despite reminders), and four were not taxpayers.
As a result, the hospice received £385 in
sponsorship and an additional of £89 in Gift Aid,
making a total of £474.

A fundraising dinner
The hospice organizes an annual dinner for one
hundred supporters, at which it normally raises
around £2,000 after paying all the costs. The dinner
tickets are £35. By splitting this into the cost of the
dinner (£20) and an optional donation (£15) and
asking people to tick the Gift Aid box, the hospice
could hope to get as much as £423 back in Gift Aid
relief. Janet ensured that this was done, and she also
had a stack of Gift Aid forms available at the dinner
for those who had forgotten to do this. The cost had
to reflect the actual cost of the dinner, and the
donation had to be optional (the supporter could
refuse to pay this, but very few ever do this).

Do this

To check out the tax
situation in your own
country get in touch with:
• The internal revenue
service.
• The body that regulates
or registers charities.
• The Council of
Voluntary Organizations
(whatever its name).
• Another charity.
• A friendly lawyer or
accountant.

What if?

You don't have charitable status

Even if your organization does not have charitable status, provided you are collecting money to support a charitable activity, there is still a way that you can claim Gift Aid. If you can find another organization that is a registered charity and ask them to receive the money, they can then claim Gift Aid and pay over the proceeds to your organization. The following might be willing to do this for you:
• A community foundation that supports good works in your area.
• A private foundation that makes charitable grants, where you know the trustees and your work falls within their terms of reference.
• A headquarters body – for example a national anorexia charity might do this for a local anorexia support group.

How to claim Gift Aid

Set yourself a target each year not just for the amount of donations you hope to raise, but also for the amount of tax you will be able to reclaim and try to persuade as many people as possible to sign Gift Aid declarations.

In order to claim Gift Aid:
• You must have charitable status. In England and Wales, this means having a charitable constitution for your organization and then registering with the Charity Commission.
• You have to register with the Inland Revenue, who will give you a Reference Number for Charity Repayment Claims.
• You have to complete a Form R68, which requires you to list the name of the donor, the date of the payment and the amount given.

Getting people to give regularly

Persuading people to give regular donations will provide you with a dependable stream of income on which you can rely for your work. There are several ways of doing this.

Standing Order or Direct Debit

Instructions are given from the donor to their bank to make regular payments, whether monthly, quarterly, annually or at any other specified interval. A Standing Order can be open-ended, so that it continues until the donor decides to stop, or it can run for a specified period, after which it ends and no further payments will be made.

With a Direct Debit, the sum paid each month can be linked to a formula, rather than being precisely the same amount. For example, it could be the cost of an annual membership subscription (which you might want to raise from time to time). To be able to use the Direct Debit scheme, you need to be a reasonably large organization. The *Charities Aid Foundation* provides a Direct Debit service for smaller charities, collecting Direct Debit donations on their behalf. You pay a set-up charge plus a fee for each Direct Debit payment.

A membership scheme

In return for certain membership benefits (such as the right to vote at an AGM, a newsletter, discounts on publications or facilities) people pay an annual (or perhaps quarterly) subscription. If these benefits are relatively small it can sometimes be paid by Gift Aid. There can be several levels of membership – 'Friend', 'Good Friend' and 'Best Friend' with subscriptions and benefits varying accordingly – and concessions for students, over-60s or family members.

A sponsorship scheme

One of the most successful schemes for regular giving is child sponsorship. For a donation of, say, 50 pence a day (this works out at around just under £235 per annum with Gift Aid relief) a person can support a child and a community in the developing world. This gives you a regular income and the donor a link between their money and the work that is being done. The donor becomes an 'investor in the child's future'.

The Payroll Giving Scheme

This enables an employee to instruct his or her employer to deduct a specified sum from his or her

Think about this

It is much easier to get someone to give £5 per month than £60 a year. Encouraging people to give more frequently can increase the amount that you raise. You might try asking for a specific amount, but suggesting that the donor chooses the frequency with which it is paid.

salary or wages each month and transfer it to a charity or charities of their choice. Many large companies use this scheme as well as some local authorities and government agencies.

Legacies and memorials

When people die, their worldly belongings (or 'estate') are distributed according to their wishes as specified in their will. People often leave money in their will to charity and for some charities this is a hugely important source of income.

A legacy to charity is Inheritance Tax-free; even if the estate is large enough to be subject to Inheritance Tax, this is not payable on any charitable bequests. The Inland Revenue is effectively contributing forty per cent of the bequest. The threshold for Inheritance Tax is reviewed in the Budget each year. In 2005-06, it was £275,000.

Different types of legacy

• A specific bequest. This is the gift of a specified asset (such as a picture or a property or shares in a company).
Advantage: the value of the item may increase over time.
Disadvantage: the item referred to may no longer belong to the deceased at the date of death or it may not be found.

• A pecuniary legacy. This is a specified sum of money.
Advantage: you know exactly how much you will get.
Disadvantage: it will decrease in value over time with inflation (around forty per cent of all Wills are over ten years old).

• The residue of an estate (or a share of it). The biggest item in many estates is property.
Advantage: the value may have increased substantially over

time (with the rise in property prices).

Disadvantage: there may be little or nothing left after the distribution of pecuniary legacies and specific bequests.

Intestacy rules

If you die without having made a will, you are said to have died 'intestate' and your property will be distributed as follows:

• If you are not married and have no relatives it will go to the Crown.

• If you have a lawful spouse (common-law partners have no rights) they will get all or a part of your estate depending on whether you have children. The amount that goes to your children is calculated according to a formula.

• If you have a lawful spouse and no children, your property will be shared between your spouse and other relatives in this order of priority: parents, siblings, grandparents, aunts and uncles. The amount that goes to your relatives is calculated according to a formula.

Intestacy means that:

• Your surviving spouse may not inherit sufficiently to maintain an adequate standard of living or to remain in the home.

• Your estate may be distributed to people who don't need it or whom you don't want to benefit.

• You may end up paying more Inheritance Tax than necessary.

How your supporters can make a charitable legacy

They can draw up a will and include a legacy specifying the charity, or leave it to their executors to decide to whom the money should go. The very big charities have legacy departments and produce guides for their donors. Remember that it is the last will that a person draws up that determines

Do this

When a Standing Order comes to an end write to the donor thanking them for their support, telling them what it has helped you to achieve and encouraging them to renew their support by signing a new Standing Order.

how their estate is distributed. If they already have a will they can add what is known as a codicil. This is a clause drawn up and witnessed in the same way as a will and which adds a further instruction to it. A codicil can be used to add a charitable bequest to an existing will without the need for rewriting the whole document.

Do this

Try to encourage the management committee of your organization and volunteers to write a will to avoid intestacy and suggest a legacy to your cause.

Memorials

A memorial gift is made by the family or a friend of the deceased to commemorate them. This can be done in one of two ways:

• A Deed of Family Arrangement. The beneficiaries and executors of the deceased effectively rewrite all or part of the will, but have to agree between themselves the variation they would like. This Deed can include a charitable legacy. This will also have the benefit of saving Inheritance Tax.

• Through their own charitable donation. This may be given using Gift Aid to save tax.

How much to ask for and how to get more

You will know how much you need from your budget calculations – whether this is your budget for a particular project, or for your organization over a three- or even five-year period. The following ideas will help you to gauge what people might be willing to donate and how to increase it:

• Never just ask for 'a generous donation', or 'whatever you can afford' – this is too vague. Always be specific.
• Do some research – you could try to find out how much they have given to other charities.
• Indicate what others are giving. People are often influenced by this, which is why it is always good to try to get some bigger donations in first.

• Explain what you need. Talk about your options for raising it and your prospects of success. Be open and honest. You might suggest that if they give a larger amount, it will help you to get larger amounts from other supporters.

• Give a range of options, linking the different amounts to various aspects of your project. Make the lowest amount low enough that people might think, 'Yes, I could give that!', but make the links with the higher amounts sound even more interesting.

• Break your total into 'bite-sized' chunks. *The Good Gifts Catalogue* (see page 84) offers people the chance to give a charitable gift in the form of a present. The catalogue contains about 100 items, each competing for the donor's attention.

• Ask for support for something very specific so that people feel they are making a real difference. With child sponsorship, for example, for just 50 pence a week, the donor is supporting a child and the local community to have a better future.

• Ask for a monthly contribution. The monthly amount will be low, but the total over the period of the gift will be quite substantial and probably be more than if the supporter had given a one-off donation.

• Offer something in return – whether an emotional incentive or some form of recognition.

Do this

If one of your committed supporters has died, why not approach the family first to ask if the will included a legacy for you. If it didn't, you might suggest the idea of a memorial? In return for their donation you could plant a tree or a flower bed, name a room or a building, or create an annual lecture in honour of the deceased.

Finding supporters

If yours is a large, successful organization with lots of existing supporters, this part of your fundraising is quite easy: invest some income in advertisements in newspapers, tens of thousands of letters in a direct mail campaign, or in PR – all of which will generate further support.

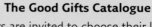

The Good Gifts Catalogue
Readers are invited to choose their level of
giving and are encouraged to give more.
And the top level is set for those who want
to mark an occasion or make a major gift.
See www.goodgifts.org
Village literacy: daily newspapers for a year
for a village library for £45; a grant to top up
the library's stock with 100 new books, £125;
a new library for a village for £1,200 to cover
furniture, books and a librarian's salary. The
money goes to the Rajiv Gandhi Foundation
Village Libraries Programme.
Blindness: gift of sight for a child, £27; gift
of sight for five people, £85; gift of sight for
100 people, £1,750. The money goes to
SightSavers to provide eye operations.
Football in Africa: three footballs for a
class, £15; ten footballs for a school, £45; to
set up a football factory providing employment to 20 young Kenyans and producing 60
balls a week, £1,000. The money goes to
Alive & Kicking, a social enterprise based in
Nairobi.

Think about this

It may be years until you
actually receive a
promised legacy but it
can mean 'life after
death' for the deceased,
in terms of keeping their
name alive, and it could
mean life for you and
your beneficiaries.

If your organization is new or just starting up, or
perhaps you have been going for some time, but
have relied on one or two big grants, how do you go
about finding new supporters?

Starting from scratch
• Hold a party or a reception at which you could
make a short presentation.

• Ask everyone connected with the organization to chip in something just to get started. Start with your founding committee and your volunteers.
• Produce a simple leaflet to tell people what you are doing, with a tear off-donations form to complete and return with their payment.
• Get publicity in the local newspaper or on local radio. If your contact details are included, people will write to you expressing their interest in helping.
• Address a local group, such as a Rotary Club or the Soroptomists. This is what Leila did (see page 30).
• Request a stand at some sort of exhibition or fair (especially if its theme is linked to what you are doing). You can hand out leaflets, engage in discussion with people who are interested and take people's business cards if they want to be kept in touch.
• Speak to everyone and anyone you meet. You're enthusiastic about what you are doing; try to inspire this in others. The more people you speak to, the more support you will gain.

If you do all of the above, you will have an ever-growing number of supporters. Aim to get ten new supporters, then twenty-five, then a hundred. Give yourself around six months to reach this target, although you may actually get there much quicker.

Widening the net

With one hundred supporters on board you may have up to £1,000–£2,000 of income coming in. You now need to:
• Make sure you get Gift Aid on as much of this income as possible (see pages 75–9).

Do this

Showing the donor exactly what their money will be spent on and that it will make a real difference to people's lives, will encourage them to give more readily and, often, to give more. Try this approach:
• This is how much it costs to restore sight to a blind person.
• This is how much it costs to keep the clinic open for a day.
• This is how much it costs to buy a much-needed piece of equipment.
• Now, how many people's sight do you wish to save, or how many days will you pay for, or will you help us to purchase the equipment we so desperately need?

• Get people to commit to give regularly using a Standing Order (see pages 78–9).
• Manage the process using some simple database software (such as 'FileMaker' or 'The Raiser's Edge').
• Maintain systems for keeping in touch (an electronic newsletter sent out quarterly – see page 51).
• Improve your promotional material – produce a really nice brochure, simple leaflets with case studies, and an annual report (see pages 35–7).
• Draft in prominent people and celebrities as patrons, who can be featured in your newsletter, attend fundraising events and provide endorsements.

Gaining more support

Your next task is to multiply the number of your supporters five- or ten-fold (the exact target will depend on the sort of organization you are and your ambitions for raising money). Here are a number of possible strategies:

• Continue with what you have been doing, but do lots more of it. Get more publicity; address many more local groups; continue to encourage people to ask friends and colleagues.
• Organize fundraising events. Sponsored walks, dinners and other entertainments all provide opportunities for raising money. These give you the opportunity to address guests of existing supporters and to tell them about your work. Ask people to leave names and contact addresses, then keep in touch with everybody who came or participated.
• If you have enough willing volunteers, organize a house-to-house or a street collection. This can

?

What if?

If I sponsor a child, what will I get in return?

Sponsor a child for just 50 pence a day and help a whole community to access the safe, clean water, healthcare and education they need to build a brighter future. You'll see the difference you're making through messages from the child you sponsor, regular updates from local fieldworkers and our supporter magazine. After all what could be a better return than knowing you've put a smile on a child's face?

Taken from an ActionAid newspaper advertisement

provide you with a good opportunity to talk to people. If anyone seems really interested, take their name and address and keep in touch with them.

• Organize an 'Open House', perhaps once a quarter, to which you invite members of the local community, politicians and others who can help you, as well as some of your more committed supporters and people you have met during the previous few months.

• Give everyone who comes into the office a leaflet and annual report and keep a visitors' book in your reception area in which people can leave their name and address.

• Put a small flyer into someone else's mailing or have it inserted into the local newspaper. This type of 'piggy-back' promotion can be quite cheap, and will spread the word much further afield.

• If any of your supporters is interested in doing a bit more, ask them to set up a small fundraising group with the task of finding supporters and raising money for you.

The number of your supporters will continue to increase; in a year or so, you will have reached your target and with 500 to 1,000 supporters, you will be in a position to become more ambitious.

Scaling up

You are now at the next stage – building your supporter base to a level where it is generating a substantial amount of income that you can rely on. How do you go about increasing the numbers further still? At this point a number of techniques become possible.

Did you know?

CRY

Rippan Kapur, an Indian airline purser, wanted to ensure that no Indian child be deprived of basic rights. He set up CRY (Child Relief and You) and he and six of his friends chipped in just about £2 each to get it going. That was the starting point for India's most successful fundraising charity, which now raises over £3 million per year.

Must know

Hitting your target

Make sure that you are targeting your approaches at the right people. For example, a local tree planting charity could approach a garden centre and ask for a leaflet to be included in their customer correspondence.

Direct mail

This involves sending unsolicited letters and leaflets to mailing lists and piggy-backing it in consumer magazines and other media.

Direct mail is really the 'junk mail' you receive in the post. It works well enough for charities, but *not that well*. You might expect to get a response rate of between one and two per cent and you will almost certainly find that your income in the early years is less than the costs that you are incurring. But the figures that matter to you are the cost of acquiring a new donor and the average 'lifetime support' that you can expect from that donor (less the cost of mailings and maintaining the database).

Street fundraising and telephone appeals

Techniques such as these tend to be expensive and unpopular with the public, although some larger charities find that they do work. If you go down this route, you should take professional advice. It is easy to commit a lot of money to this sort of fundraising and end up disappointed.

Getting plenty of publicity for what you are doing

• Apply for a BBC television (monthly) or radio appeal (weekly) slot. You need to demonstrate that there is public interest in what you are doing. For further information, see www.bbc.co.uk/info/policies/charities. Also contact your local television and radio stations (both the BBC and independent networks) to see if they will do a feature around your work.
• Organize events that bring you a lot of publicity – such as conferences, publications, launches, stunts. And make sure that the media hear about what you are doing and report on it.
• Employ a PR agency to get publicity for you. This can be extremely cost-effective if what you are doing is 'newsworthy'.

Beware of potential pitfalls

As your organization grows, there will be some potential pitfalls. Being aware of them, however, should help you to avoid them:

• Your organization starts to develop as a bureaucracy – your budget, your fundraising targets, the next big grant all begin to assume more importance than the work you were set up to do.

• You begin to lose the enthusiasm and commitment that were so important to you when you started out.

• You take on fundraising staff at considerable expense and perhaps they are not that good.

• You spend too much on fundraising, you find it difficult to generate the sums you need, it becomes a bit of a treadmill, staggering from one year to the next to keep your balance sheet in the black.

   If any of these happen, go back to basics and remind yourself why you started campaigning in the first place. Visit some recipients of help from your organization to help you rearrange your priorities again.

Recognizing supporters' generosity

People are often encouraged to give money if there is some form of recognition involved. You might:

• Display their name on a board listing all your donors and patrons in your entrance lobby.

• Include their name in a programme or annual report.

• Get publicity for the donation (if it is sufficiently important) in the local newspaper, perhaps with a photograph of the cheque being handed over.

• Name an event or activity after them, such as an annual lecture.

• Plant a tree or a garden in their honour.

• Name a room or a building after them if they've made a very large donation.

Did you know?

Amnesty

Amnesty started as a result of publicity in a national newspaper. Peter Benenson, a lawyer, read an article about two Portuguese students who had been imprisoned for drinking a toast to freedom. He wrote an article about this in the *Observer* inviting people to join him in taking action. The response was enormous. The rest is history.

Techniques for asking effectively

When it comes to doing the asking, here are some
key principles:

• Always ask nicely, of course, but be assertive at the
same time. If you are determined enough, you will
get many more people to give to you.

• Don't be embarrassed to ask. You're not just there for
a chat; you need to 'close the deal' by actually asking.

• Decide how much you want and ask for it, but always
have a fallback position so that if someone turns down
your first request, you can then suggest, say, that they
pay the same sum over a period of time, or perhaps a
smaller amount.

• If you lack the power of persuasion, try asking someone
else to do it for you.

The role of Trustees in fundraising

Most Trustees don't expect to give, and they would run a mile if
you asked them to ask others to give. But it is good to get everyone
at the head of the organization to give something – whether money
or professional skills (which you can put a value on). This will create
a culture of fundraising within the organization.

Having a Development Committee

You may want to establish a separate Development Committee,
whose members will help you to raise money.

It is important that:

• Development Committee members share your vision and values.

• Committee members provide access to all the sectors you want
to approach – local people, the business community, government,
the very wealthy, freemasons, Rotarians, churches, foundations,
rock stars.

• The Committee Chairperson has good leadership skills.

• A target is agreed with the Committee for the amount to be raised.

> **Urban Trust**
>
> Peter was having only limited success raising money for the Urban Trust to set up social and economic regeneration projects for ethnic minorities following a series of race riots. He had one good contact – the Managing Director of a leading insurance company of which the Chairman was a leading light in *Business in the Community*. He managed to get a ten-minute meeting with the Chairman, who not only agreed to give, but also agreed to send a short handwritten covering letter with a simple brochure to twenty business leaders, which said: 'This is a really interesting project. We're giving £10,000 to it, will you support it too?' The outcome was seven donations of between £5,000 and £10,000. A really productive ten minutes!

• Committee members are happy to provide a list of their contacts, and then approach them.

• There is good administrative back-up so that people can do the asking with relative ease. This might include some induction, help with fixing up appointments and providing support materials.

Organizing a large fundraising appeal

There may come a time when you need to raise a great deal of money – for example to purchase or repair a building, or to buy equipment. What do you do? Here is a simple step-by-step guide.

Step 1: Think about what you want to do and why you want to do it

• Have a collective think-in. Share ideas.

• Talk to someone who has done it before and can offer you the benefit of their experience.

• Decide whether you *really* want to do it. It will require a lot of time and effort.

Must know

Collecting law

Ensure that you comply with the law on public collections. This sets out how you should run the collection and how you must account for the money.

Step 2: Plan how you are going to set about it
• Work out a budget for how much you need.
• Work out how much time you have – the longer, the better, but there are sometimes circumstances where you need to respond very quickly.
• Think about where the money is going to come from. This might include: money you will borrow from the bank or a wealthy supporter; money you will raise in big grants from the government or the lottery; what you are expecting foundations, business and individuals to give.

Work out the total for each source, plus the number of donations and the amounts of each. For example, to raise £40,000 from individuals, you might plan to get: one donation of £5,000; four donations of £2,500; five donations of £1,000; twenty donations of £500; one hundred donations of £100.

This is your plan; it provides you with a challenge for your fundraising. You have to go out and find the 130 people you need – by giving talks, making presentations, approaching government bodies, charitable foundations and companies, encouraging your contacts to support the appeal.

Step 3: The preparatory stage
Before you formally launch the appeal you will need to:
• Put in place a 'Leadership Group' (this includes an Appeal Committee) of people who can give and who have good contacts; and a Patron – a celebrity or someone who is well respected.
• Prepare presentation materials, including a brochure and a short video to show at meetings.
• Secure your 'lead grants' – the success of your appeal may depend on one or more large grants, so get pledges for these before going any further.
• Get any permissions you need (such as Planning Permission).
• Develop your PR plans for a public launch.

Step 4: The public launch
• Announce your appeal, and put your plans into action. This involves meeting, talking to and persuading people to support you. Encourage people to give generously: 'So-and-so has agreed to give £1,000. Why don't you...'. Or, 'If you can't afford £100, why not give £25 a year for four years?'
• Activate your Appeal Committee. Discuss with each person who to approach and how much to ask for. Set targets for how much they will bring in.
• Organize celebrations when you reach particular milestones and use these to thank people who have given and inspired others to give.

Step 5: Close the appeal
You've got there. You've raised the amount you need. Publicize your success and make sure that everyone is thanked – all those who gave and helped to make the appeal a success.

Collecting from the public
There are a number of ways of doing this.

House-to-house collections
Try knocking on people's doors armed with leaflets and donations forms. Ask for money there and then, offer to call back the next day when they have had time to read the information and consider the cause or simply leave the information in the hope that they will reply if they want to support you. House-to-house collections are a good tool for local charities, letting you introduce yourself to people as part of the community, invite them to visit you and see your work or ask them to local events.

Street collections and flag days
Collect in the street, giving a 'flag' or a sticker to anyone who gives you money, as with 'Poppy Day' or 'Alexandra Rose Day'.

Must know

Legal issues

Public collections (in the street or door-to-door) in the UK are regulated by the Charities Act 1992. But new provisions were introduced in the Charities Bill, which became law in 2006. Under the new rules, no permit is needed for house-to-house collections, but the local authority must be notified in advance. When collecting in a public place, the charity should obtain a Public Collections Certificate from the Charity Commission (which can be issued for up to five years). They can refuse to grant this certificate on several grounds, including that an insufficient proportion of the proceeds will actually reach the charity. A permit must also be obtained from the local council but can only be refused on the grounds of inconvenience.

Bucket collections

Many charities organize these at supermarkets, cinemas, outside football stadiums and other venues where people are enjoying themselves. Students do the same on 'rag days' in the street, on public transport, and at railway stations, often in fancy dress. Using some sort of sealed collecting device is preferable to an open bucket, so that all the money collected can be properly accounted for.

Static collecting devices

Placed in a prominent public place, such as outside a shop or in a theatre (with the owner's permission), these can be quite successful, particularly if they have lots of 'bells and whistles' to attract attention.

Collecting boxes on shop counters

Small shops and pubs are often happy to place a collecting box on the counter, so that people can donate their loose change. Ensure that your boxes are attractive and well-positioned and that you remember to empty them from time to time.

Collecting boxes in people's homes

People often keep these on a mantelpiece or by the phone for their own or their visitors' loose change.

Making the most of your collection

Once you have decided to organize a collection, the challenge is to see how to raise even more money from it. Here are some ideas:

• Find really good sites – places where there are lots of people passing, and at times when they are not feeling too rushed.

• Use as many collectors as possible – the more you have, the more money you will collect.

• Collect in good weather – if there is a biting wind or if it's pouring with rain people won't be in the mood to support you.

• Recruit volunteers who are personable and enthusiastic – ensure that they make eye contact and smile and also that they know all they need to about your organization.

• Provide some explanatory literature for those who want to know more.

• Ask people to sign a Gift Aid form (see pages 75–9) if they give £1 or more. This will add twenty-eight per cent to the value of the donation.

• Keep a record of all the money collected, and pay it into a bank account as soon as possible. You need to conduct your collection properly if you are to maintain people's confidence in your organization and its work.

• Debrief after the event – make a record of all the points raised so that next time you can do it even better.

• Thank all your volunteers – and tell them how successful your collection has been; this will encourage them to help again next time.

• Put names and addresses on your mailing list and keep in regular contact with those who gave them.

Want to know more?

To purchase collecting boxes and other fundraising materials, contact:
• Angal Services to Fundraisers: 91 Ewell Road, Surbiton KT6 6AH (020 8390 9393) www.angal.co.uk Email sales@angal.co.uk
• ECL Plastics, 3 Richmond Road, Trafford Park, Manchester M17 1RE (0161 877 8333) www.eclplastics.co.uk
• The Institute of Fundraising keeps a list of professional fundraisers: www.institute-of-fundraising.org.uk

5 Raising money through fundraising activities

From the obvious to the less obvious, this chapter explains how to run successful events that raise money for your charity. It covers everything from arranging advertising so that enough people turn up, to insuring outdoor events against a sudden downpour.

Choosing your method

The fundraising method you choose should be appropriate for the type of people you identified as your target audience, so think about this carefully before you start.

Must know

Charity ribbons

• For a list of ribbon colours and causes, visit: http://kiwijewels.com/ awareness_colors_and_ meanings.htm
• For directions on how to make charity ribbons visit www.cancer.org /docroot/gi/content/ GI_2_5_Make_Pink_ Ribbon_Pin_Directions. asp

Ribbons and wristbands

Ribbons are used by lots of causes as symbols for promoting awareness. Organize a 'ribbon week' in the office, at school or elsewhere in the community to raise consciousness.

One of the best-known ribbon campaigns is the red ribbon used to promote HIV/AIDS awareness. Others include pink (for breast cancer) and gold (childhood cancer).

Lance Armstrong's 'Livestrong' campaign for cancer survivors, run in association with Nike, made wristbands 'the new ribbons' for people to show solidarity with a cause. Today wristbands are produced in the whole spectrum of colours for all sorts of causes.

'Beat Bullying' was an anti-bullying campaign run in 2004 by BBC Radio 1 and the UK Department for Education and Skills. They produced a bright blue wristband for young people to wear in solidarity with the campaign and got celebrities such as Wayne Rooney, Rio Ferdinand, Scissor Sisters and Franz Ferdinand to support the campaign by wearing one. This created a huge demand for the wristbands, not all of which could be met; they became so popular that some were being traded for up to £30 on eBay, and, it was reported, some pupils even resorted to bullying to obtain them from other children!

Collecting and recycling to raise money

Collecting old mobile phones

The average handset is replaced every eighteen months; over 15 million mobile phones are replaced in the UK each year. Some are traded in (usually as part of a special promotion to encourage customers to upgrade), but many are just forgotten about or thrown away.

Handsets are designed to last for between seven and ten years; in developing countries, there is a demand for cheap handsets (mobile phone use is booming all over the world) and having the latest model is not so important.

Here are two recycling schemes:

Community Fonebak (www.communityfone bak.com) will pay you £4 cash or give you a £5 Dixons voucher (which can be spent in Dixons, Currys, The Link or PC World) for each phone that can be resold. The scheme is open to any organization in the UK or Ireland, including registered charities, schools, scout troops, and sports clubs. To join you just need a bank account with two signatories.

Cellular Surplus (www.cellular-surplus.com) will partner you to design and organize a community recycling scheme for mobile phones, with the proceeds going to your charity.

Collecting inkjet and toner cartridges

These schemes are similar to the mobile phone schemes.

Recycle4charity will donate 60 pence per inkjet cartridge you collect to a nominated charity. You can register your own charity and nominate yourselves

Do this

If you have enough keen supporters, produce a wristband that you can sell for between £1.50 and £2. Try to get a celebrity to wear your wristband – this sort of publicity will make it a 'cool' fashion accessory that others will want to buy and wear.
You can find wristband suppliers on Google.

Do this

Approach local companies and ask if they will donate their used cartridges to your collection scheme. If they aren't collecting for somebody else, they may be happy to do this. Approach the office manager in the first instance.

as recipients. This is an initiative of Donate As You Spend (DAYS): www.days.org.uk.

Environmental Protection Services will donate 50 pence for each printer cartridge you collect (excludes Epson) to a charity you nominate: www.environ mentalprotectionservices.org.

Collecting small change

Ask your supporters to collect their small change for you – and you can do this yourself. Buy a tall spaghetti jar and empty all your small change (1p, and 2p, 5p, 10p, 20p and perhaps even 50p pieces) into it. It mounts up very quickly and with just twenty people collecting, say, an average of £50 a year, £1,000 is raised with virtually no effort at all. Why not keep a collecting jar in your toilet at home and invite guests to contribute some loose change every time they visit?

Lotteries, raffles and tombolas

A lottery is the distribution of prizes by chance. People pay for a ticket in order to participate. A proportion of the money generated will go to good causes, while the rest covers the administration costs and provides a profit for the lottery operator.

Here are some of the different types of lottery:

• **Lotteries** – where the prizes are usually cash. The largest lottery is the National Lottery promoted by the government. There are international lotteries such as Il Gordo (the fat one), the Spanish lottery run by ONCE (the Spanish Association for the Blind) and Euro-Millions, which is a collaboration of lottery operators in nine European countries.

- **Raffles** – where the prizes are usually in kind (such items as cases of wine, holidays, free meals in restaurants, etc.).
- **Tombolas** – where every ticket wins a prize. Your ticket is numbered, and your ticket number determines the prize you get. Prizes vary in value but because you are certain of winning something, tombola tickets are usually sold for a higher price than raffle tickets.
- **Scratchcards** – where you scratch the surface of the lottery ticket to see if you have won.
- **Sweepstakes** – where each entrant puts up a stake and draws a horse in a horserace. The winning ticket 'sweeps all stakes' – that is, it wins the lot. Many charities and workplaces organize a sweepstake on the Grand National steeplechase, which is run in the UK each spring.
- **Hundred clubs** – where one hundred members contribute a sum monthly into a draw. Each month a winning ticket is drawn, and a proportion goes to the winner and the rest to the charity.
- **Games of skill** – where more than chance is required. An entry fee is charged for participating. Sometimes, the games involve real skill, such as a really difficult quiz, but in other cases the questions require very little skill, which makes the game a virtual lottery, but one that may fall outside your country's gaming regulations.
- **Free entry games**. Many sales promotions are games of skill, but with free entry, for example a premium telephone line quiz, where a part of the cost of your telephone call goes to the organizer, which pays for the prize, and in some cases can generate a huge profit.

Must know

Permissions

Depending upon the nature of your event, you may need some sort of licence (to run the event, collect money in a public place, run a bar or have dancing). Before you get down to any detailed planning find out what licences you need, how long they will take to get and what they will cost.

Must know

UK law

The legislation regulating gaming in the UK is the Gambling Act 2005. This came fully into force in 2007.
www.gamblingcommission.gov.uk

These are the requirements in the UK for registering your lottery:
• Small lotteries (one-off events with prizes up to the value of £250) do not need to register.
• Private lotteries – not-for-profit lotteries may be run within any environment and do not need to register.
• Society lotteries with proceeds in a single lottery of over £20,000, or with cumulative annual proceeds of more than £250,000 must be registered either with the Gambling Commission or the local authority, depending on the level of ticket sales. Charities using lotteries or scratchcards to raise substantial sums of money may find that they need to register. No licence is needed for a raffle held as part of a dance or similar event, where the draw takes place at the end; nor is one needed for a draw or sweepstake in the workplace, provided tickets are sold to fellow employees only.

How to run a raffle

Here are some guidelines for running a raffle, whether it is linked to another fundraising event, or an initiative in its own right.

Step 1: Ascertain whether you need to register. For most raffles, the answer is likely to be 'No'.

Step 2: Set up an organizing group. One person will be the 'promoter' of the raffle, and be responsible for seeing that it is a success.

Step 3: Plan your raffle. How many prizes will you need? What price will the tickets be? (Key factors here are the price per ticket, and the price of a book of five or ten which you can offer at a discount.) How many do you hope to sell? When will the draw be held?

Step 4: Get prizes donated. Try to get a few really fabulous prizes such as a holiday for two in an exotic location, or money-can't-buy 'dreams' and 'promises' that will catch people's imagination.

Then you can get lots of other things donated – a case or bottles of wine from a wine merchant; a meal for two at a local restaurant; or a hamper of nice things to eat from a deli. Just ring round and ask.

Step 5: Print the tickets. Type 'raffle tickets' into Google, and lots of specialist printers will appear. On the tickets highlight some of the prizes, print the price and give the promoter's name and address. Have three times as many tickets printed as you think will need – sales might go better than you think. If the raffle is organized as part of an event, you will be selling the tickets at the event, and you can use simple numbered cloakroom tickets.

Step 6: Sell the tickets. Ask your volunteers and supporters to sell tickets for you; encourage them to take a number of books to sell to their friends and colleagues. Try to get some publicity.

Organizing an auction

An auction is like a raffle in that prizes are donated, but instead of putting them into a lottery, you auction them off. It can make for an entertaining fundraising

> **Did you know?**
>
> **Lottery income**
>
> Society lotteries in the UK generate some £140 million a year of income, with £75 million going to charity.

evening, either on its own or linked to a dinner or reception.

A successful auction needs:

• A lively outgoing person with a sense of humour to act as auctioneer – someone who can 'work the crowd', possibly a professional auctioneer (many are happy to donate their services) or an actor.

• Lots of people to come and bid.

• An interesting venue – somebody's home, the top floor of the 'Gherkin' (the City of London's landmark skyscraper), a club, a smart hotel ...

• A good atmosphere, so that people feel extra generous.

• Lots of desirable things to auction; try to match these with the audience – are they art lovers, wine drinkers, football fans?

Auctions of promises or dreams

Besides asking for people to give you things, you can ask them to donate their talents or to use their position or contacts to provide a special opportunity that could be auctioned.

In an auction of promises there might be a promise to mow the winner's lawn once a week for three months or babysit five times, for example. An auction of dreams would offer things that money can't buy, such as dinner for two with a famous pop star; a week at someone's fabulous holiday home; watching a football match from the dugout.

Hold an auction on eBay

If you don't know how eBay works, there are simple instructions on the website on how to buy and sell. There are also some good guidebooks that take you through the whole process. In the UK, eBay has a 'charity page' on which charities can promote their auctions.

The Great Chicago Fire eBay Sale was an eBay auction organized by the Chicago municipality to raise money for the arts. Items donated included a 1960s Playboy bunny costume, a dinner party prepared by the personal chef to Oprah Winfrey, the opportunity to dye the Chicago River green and much more.

The PhotoVoice Photography eBay auction in 2006 sold over one hundred prints donated by leading photographers to support the organization PhotoVoice, which teaches photography to street children and refugees.

Entertainment events

An entertainment event provides you with an opportunity to reach out to people whose interest lies in attending your event rather than supporting your cause but who may become interested through participating and hearing about what you are doing.

There are all sorts of entertainment events you can organize to raise money, including: sporting events and tournaments, musical and cultural events (art exhibitions, film premières and concerts), balls, fashion shows, discos for young people, and so on.

The benefits of an event include:
- The money that is pledged and raised.
- Deepening the relationship with existing volunteers and supporters who attend.
- Attracting new people and therefore new support. As always, keep a note of everyone who attends and write to them thanking them for participating, enclosing a leaflet or newsletter with which you can include a request for support.
- Good publicity is being generated for your organization and its work, which will help to build your reputation.
- You may develop relationships with celebrities whom you can contact in the future to help with other fundraising activities.

Tip

Keep it simple

Start by organizing something simple. Leave the more complicated, bigger and more risky events for when you have had experience that you can build upon.

How to organize a successful event

Here's a checklist of all the things you need to do in order to organize a successful event.

1. Decide what type of event you want to organize.

2. Define your objectives – list up to three main objectives for your event and be as specific as you can about what you want to get out of it.

3. Work out who you need to have in your organizing team and what each of their particular responsibilities will be: a treasurer to keep track of the money; a publicist to promote the event and get people to come; an editor to write all the publicity materials; a designer to design the posters, programme and banners; an organizer to plan the event and co-ordinate the team of volunteers; a fundraiser to plan how to get the most money from the event and to get advertising for the programme and sponsorship for the event as a whole; a leader to be responsible for the whole thing.

4. Agree a budget for the event. Make an estimate of all the costs you might incur and think about how you will cover them. Keep your costs as low as possible – it is far easier to spend money than it is to raise it!

5. Give the event a catchy title.

6. Decide who you would like to come to the event – your donors perhaps, your members, your volunteers, your newsletter readers? Or do you want to reach out to a wider audience?

7. Think about how you are going to reach people (publicity in the local paper or on local radio, posters in pubs and shops, word of mouth, via other networks and organizations, and so on)?

8. Decide on a venue (see page 109).

9. Fix a date for the event sooner rather than later and plan well ahead. The more time you allow yourself, the easier it will be to make the event a success.

10. Plan a programme. If it's an annual event, you should look at previous years to see what needs improving.

11. Think about any speakers and celebrities you might want to approach and find out how to do so.

12. Ascertain whether you need any official permissions or insurance cover. (You should be able to check this out with the venue.)

13. Think about any props and equipment you will need. Will you need chairs or tables and if so, how many? Will you buy these, or rent them? (If you have storage space it may well be cheaper to buy them and use them for subsequent events.)

14. If there are going to be refreshments, decide who will provide them and what you will charge for them.

15. Organize any posters, banners, decorations, t-shirts or armbands for helpers and publicity material that you need (including leaflets for distribution at the actual event). Who will be responsible for producing these?

16. Work out how many helpers you are going to need on the day and what their specific tasks will be. Who will be responsible for briefing and co-ordinating them?

17. Minimize the risk – one way of doing this is to get all (or as many as possible) of the costs paid for by a sponsor. Another is to get guarantees from supporters for the number of tickets that they will take and sell before you decide to go ahead.

Must know

Draw up a budget

Your budget must include:
- Cost of the venue.
- Equipment hire, such as sound systems, lighting.
- Decoration of the stage or the hall, including flowers, banners and displays.
- Performers' fees and expenses (travel, accommodation, meals); this should be confirmed in a formal letter.
- Printing costs (for tickets, programmes and any other PR material).
- Any costs of selling the tickets (you may offer a commission to sell tickets, or a discount for bulk purchase).
- Stewards and others needed on the day and their expenses.
- Administration and support costs; this might include a fee to an event organizer for a particularly large or complicated event.
- Sundry and contingency – a budget for the unexpected – you will usually need it!

Must know

'Go green days'

Office workers or students are asked to turn up dressed all in green and to contribute £1 to your environmental project. There may be a competition for the best fancy dress and you could even think about levying a £2 fine for all of those not wearing green.

Linking events and causes

Consider whether there might be a natural link between an event and the work that you are doing. SightSavers, for example, organized a blind golf tournament in Kenya, which not only highlighted their work with the blind but also showed the blind in an extremely positive light.

Hunger banquets

Invite about twenty people, each of whom is randomly assigned to a group as follows: fifteen per cent are in the high-income group – they sit at a table and enjoy a three-course meal; twenty-five per cent are in the middle-income group – they sit on chairs and eat rice and beans; the remaining sixty per cent represent the world's poor – they sit on the floor and get only rice and water. They will be suffering the fate of the billions of poor people throughout the world who are undernourished and go to bed hungry each night. Use a hunger banquet to raise money to fight global poverty. Make sure that you make the rich pay more! Find out more from Oxfam America: www.hungerbanquet.org and www.oxfamamerica.org.

Chain dinners

Invite twelve people to dinner and ask each of them for a fiver. Pay for the food yourself and encourage at least three of the people who have come to your dinner to organize their own dinner in the same way. They then ask three more people and you will have started a chain dinner.

Speed dating (for safe motherhood!)

Maternity Worldwide encourages its supporters to organize speed dating evenings to raise money. The general idea is that participants spend three to five minutes with the person next to them, then a buzzer sounds and they move on to the next person. Each person is given a Speed Dating card and ticks the names of people they would like to see again. If ticks are mutual, then they will be sent their new friends' e-mail addresses. What happens next is up to them! The website www.maternityworldwide.org gives instructions.

Quiz evenings

Check out www.millionquestionquiz.com which has lots of questions you can use, and a function that allows you to organize a sponsored quiz competition with participants raising money based on the number of questions they are able to answer correctly. The website www.wizardtrivia.com also has quiz questions that are available on a subscription basis.

Choosing the right venue

Your choice of venue is really important. When you visit potential venues, keep the following in mind:
• Is it available on the date you need it?
• How will your event run (including factors such as where the registration desk will be, where the performers will change, where drinks will be served, how the seating will be arranged, the audio-visual facilities, and so on)?
• Size – ensure that it is neither too small nor too large.
• It should be easily accessible with reasonably good transport links, parking facilities and disability access.
• What facilities and services are provided and/or included in the price? You may have to pay Value Added Tax or even a Service Charge in addition to the quoted fee.
• What are the cancellation terms?
• Are there any restrictions on usage?
• You may be required to use a particular caterer, so find out about the catering costs.

Covering all eventualities – what if ...

... it rains non-stop all day?
Plan a contingency for adverse weather. And consider getting insurance for this sort of thing (see page 121).

... your volunteer team loses interest?
Make sure everyone involved is committed. Talk through all the potential pitfalls and less-than favourable outcomes so that they know what to expect.

... you miss the deadline for getting into the 'What's On' section of the local newspaper?
Making a publicity plan and schedule should ensure that everything is done on time and that this doesn't happen!

... the venue is booked?
If you think you've found the ideal venue but it's unavailable on the date you want, it might be worth changing the date of your event rather than looking for another venue.

... your star guest's agent calls two hours before the event demanding a huge fee?
Remember to confirm all arrangements in writing, so you can point out that it was agreed that you would only pay travel expenses, for example. Point out the terrible publicity that the celebrity would get if they failed to turn up.

... only twenty-five per cent of the tickets are sold with one week to go?
• Think about whether anyone might buy a large number of tickets for distribution to their employees or to enable children from a local school to attend.
• Give free tickets to people who would like to come, but can't afford to do so (schoolchildren, pensioners, hospital workers, etc.) – if you can't sell the tickets, it is better for seats to be filled than empty.
• Run a last-minute advertisement in the local paper saying that there are free tickets for the first hundred people who turn up.

A sample event from start to finish

You are planning an 'Evening of Magic', involving a well-known magician called Hey Presto. You have run something like this before and it went well, so you are confident that you will be able to repeat this success. Mr Presto's agent asked for a fee of £750 plus travel expenses for both the magician and his assistant, explaining that this was just 50 per cent of the usual appearance fee because it was for charity. Consider this in the context of your budget: if you hope to raise £15,000, then this sort of fee is fine, but if you will be struggling to raise even £1,000, it will eat up most of your income. You must also check

Must know

Celebrity involvement

Celebrities can really transform an event – if the right celebrity is involved it will encourage people to attend, make them feel good when they are there, and will certainly get you media publicity.

what their expenses are likely to be and whether VAT will be charged.

Next you need a venue. You want somewhere that will seat 150 people. The choice is between a community hall with basic facilities that will cost you £100, and a posh stately home costing £550 including chair hire. This is a big decision. Whilst the cost is an important consideration, you also want the right setting and ambience for your evening. You decide to go for the stately home and to charge just a little bit more for the tickets.

You now need to price the tickets. These, you decide, will not be too expensive, but you will also organize a charity auction during the evening to raise a bit more money. You price the tickets at £15 for adults, £10 for children, with twenty-five 'premium tickets' in the front rows selling for £25. If you sell all the tickets, you will raise £2,250. Before you make the final decision to proceed, you ask ten of your keen supporters if they would each agree to purchase eight tickets and either use them themselves or sell them. This will underwrite the cost of the evening, and ensure that you won't make a loss.

You need a printed programme for the evening, and you decide to try to sell advertising space, charging £50 for a quarter page – this will more than cover the costs of producing the programme.

Next, ask your team of volunteers to do the following:
• Arrange for gifts to be donated by local shops and supporters for the auction; you will ask a group of three people to do this.
• Make arrangements for handling and accounting for the money; your Treasurer will agree to do this.

• Publicize the event, so that all the tickets are sold, and ensure that a photographer comes from the local newspaper; the person who does all of this will also be responsible for getting tickets printed and seeing that appropriate publicity material is distributed on the evening.

• Make all the on-the-ground arrangements at the venue.

• Deal with Mr Presto and find an auctioneer – which you will do yourself, along with co-ordinating the team of volunteers and being responsible for ensuring the overall success of the event.

Working with celebrities

Involving the right celebrity in an event can make all the difference – it will encourage people to come along, give the event that 'feelgood' factor and most certainly help with media coverage. But how do you approach them? Here are some ideas:

• If you personally know a celebrity who would be right for your event, ask them if they would be willing to participate. If they are busy on the date in question, it might be worth changing the date to fit around their schedule. You can also ask your supporters, volunteers or committee members if they know anyone who might be your celebrity.

• Write to one or two people out of the blue, probably via their agent, and follow up your letter with a telephone call.

• Go to where you know the person in question will be – wait at the stage door for an actor or musician and ask to visit their dressing room to tell them how much you liked the show. Don't be afraid to ask.

• Most celebrities you approach will suggest you write to their agent or manager. But this existing (albeit small) first point of contact with them should help to get their agent to take your request seriously.

Did you know?

'Click and Donate' sites are one of the most successful forms of website sponsorship, whereby the sponsor pays a small cash sum for each visitor clicking an icon. The best examples are www.therainforest site.com where each click preserves one square metre of rainforest, and www.thehungersite.com where a click provides a meal for a hungry person.

Do this

When dealing with celebrities:
• Get something in writing from them confirming that they will attend.
• Make sure they are well briefed – they need to know exactly what they are expected to do and a little about what you are raising money for.
• Make sure there are adequate toilet and dressing room facilities for their comfort. Put flowers in their dressing room (at an event).
• Delegate somebody to meet and greet them and to provide them with whatever they need.
• Publicly thank them for the wonderful job they've done and arrange for a child to hand them a bouquet.
• Write and thank them afterwards and tell them how much money they helped you to raise. Include a photograph of them.

What makes a good celebrity?

The right celebrity for the event is the one who will appeal to your audience. Omar Sharif, for example, is a fantastic bridge player (as well as Dr Zhivago!) and would be a wonderful draw for a bridge evening. Andy Flintoff, who hit Australia for six to win the Ashes, would appeal to almost everybody.

Celebrity status might be broken down as follows:
• **A-list:** TV soap stars; Olympic gold medallists; international celebrities such as Madonna or Bob Geldof; the Prime Minister or the Queen (but royal protocol can be a real problem).
• **B-list:** well-known TV presenters; famous theatre actors; senior cabinet ministers; the Archbishop of Canterbury.
• **C-list:** a drummer in a well-known band; your local MP; best-selling authors; minor royals.
• **D-list:** the Mayor or Leader of the Council; anyone who was B-List fifteen years ago; the managing director of the local big business; a 'Lord' or 'Lady'.

Participation events

In this type of event, people take part in some sort of challenge and collect money from friends and colleagues for completing it. For example:
• A sponsored cycle ride, perhaps over 30km, 50km or even 80km; participants are sponsored for each kilometre they complete or for the ride as a whole.
• A sponsored run – perhaps a marathon (where people train hard to compete) or a much shorter 'fun run' in fancy dress; a variation is a relay marathon, where a team of, say, eight people complete a marathon between them.

• Something more dangerous or challenging, such as parachuting or abseiling.
• Challenge activities, such as cycling the Great Wall of China, or walking the Pennine Way, or climbing Mount Everest.
• Something directly related to the cause, such as a sponsored litter pick for an environmental campaign.

The event has to be appropriate to the age and interests of participants. If students or teenagers are involved, for example, a dance marathon (non-stop dancing through the night), whereby they are sponsored for each hour they stay on their feet, might appeal. A health charity might organize a sponsored stop-smoking initiative, where participants get sponsorship for each day they continue not to smoke (say, up to a limit of thirty days, as the event has to have an end).

To ensure the success of these events you need to:
• Round up participants – the more the better.
• Get each participant to commit to raising a certain minimum sum (you provide sponsorship forms, publicity material and encouragement); you could think about offering a prize for the person who raises the most.
• Possibly ask participants to pay an entry fee, depending on the nature of the event; then for a sponsored parachute jump you might require the participant to raise at least four times the cost of making the jump in order not to have to pay to participate.
• Make sure that participants collect the money pledged as quickly as possible after the event (certainly within one month).

Must know

Spend wisely

Keep your costs as low as possible – ask for discounts wherever you can and get as much as possible donated. In order to make your event look good and to appear well organized, however, it may be worth 'investing' in certain things, such as decorating the venue and having efficient, smartly turned out stewards, to give the event an edge.

Think about this

- If your chosen celebrity demands a fee, are you prepared to pay it? The right celebrity may help to generate significantly more funding and publicity – if paying the fee creates too much financial risk, you could consider getting sponsorship.
- If they demand 'star' treatment (such as staying in a five-star hotel overnight and being fetched by a stretch limo) are you prepared to go along with this? Every pound you spend on them is one less for the cause.

Organizing a sponsored event

A successful sponsored event must be carefully planned from start to finish. You'll have to make the following decisions:
- What type of event do you want to organize?
- When should it be held?
- How much do you want to raise?
- How many people are going to participate?
- What sort of people will participate?
- Will there be an entry fee for participants?
- What is the minimum sponsorship you expect from each participant?
- What is the 'unit of sponsorship' (circuits, miles, kilometres, hours etc.)?
- How will you get people to sign up?

Division of labour

You will need a team to deal with the following:
- **Treasury**: banking the funds raised and seeing that donations are Gift Aided wherever possible.
- **Logistics:** staking out the course and putting up signage where necessary (including signposting toilet facilities); ensuring food and water are available; briefing the celebrity who will launch the event; arranging completion certificates for all participants; recruiting and briefing a small team of volunteers to act as stewards and helpers on the day.
- **Promotion:** marketing the event to people who might be interested in participating; preparing briefing packs and sponsorship forms for participants; providing an information stall at the finish; getting publicity; producing banners, placards and t-shirts.

Case study

Ravenswood, a home for people with learning disabilities (now merged with Norwood: Children and Families First), pioneered the concept of fundraising challenge events with its cycle ride from Dan to Beersheva in the 1990s, when 150 riders raised over £500,000. Today many leading charities organize their own fundraising challenges.

The 2006 Norwood Challenges included cycling and trekking across the party island of Lanzarote, a 450km ride through Kerala in South India, and a Golf Aid challenge playing 90 holes over five courses in one day!

Marie Curie Cancer Care organized a cycle ride for 500 people 'to raise millions for cancer care'. Riders started from five different cities (Krakow, Berlin, Gdansk, Prague and Vilnius) cycling from 50-75 miles per day and converging on Warsaw, the birthplace of Marie Curie. Participants had to pay a registration fee of £235 and pledge to raise a minimum of £1,450 in sponsorship (of which at least £1,100 would go to the charity, after expenses).

• **Participant support:** keeping in touch with all participants to ensure that they are happy with their progress in finding sponsors; providing them with advice if they are finding it harder than they thought to get sponsors; meeting and briefing them on the day; contacting them after the event to ensure they collect all the money pledged by their sponsors.

• **Organization:** co-ordinating the team and taking the lead role for ensuring that it is a success; dealing with legal and contractual matters, such as permission to use a park or public liability insurance.

After the event

Naturally everyone should be written to and thanked – sponsors and participants alike. You can supply the

Must know

Sponsorship forms

All participants must be provided with sponsorship forms, so that people sponsoring them can pledge support. The forms should include the following information: the name of the sponsor, the amount they are pledging, their signature and their contact details.

thank-you letters for participants to send to their sponsors or you can ask them for contact details and send the letters out from your office.

Thanking people also provides you with the opportunity to ask for additional support. You can:

• Add the names and addresses of participants and their sponsors to your mailing list, and when you thank them ask them to tell you if they would rather not receive information from your organization.

• Ask all the sponsors as well as all the participants if they would like to participate in next year's fun event.

• Tell participants and their sponsors what their money and effort has helped you to achieve and ask whether they might consider becoming regular supporters.

Justgiving

Creating a personal fundraising page on the Justgiving.com website is a really easy way of collecting sponsorship. Simply go to the Justgiving website (www.justgiving.com), select a charity, add a photo and a message, then e-mail this to everyone you know. Put the weblink on any promotional material you use to get sponsorship.

Pledges can be paid by credit or debit card from anywhere in the world and an e-mail receipt will follow. Justgiving sends your donations directly to your charity's bank account (which is a guarantee against loss or fraud) and automatically reclaims twenty-eight per cent extra in Gift Aid tax relief on donations made by UK taxpayers. They charge a small transaction fee (currently five per cent of the gross donation), but the fee you pay will be far less than the Gift Aid reclaimed. It's a simple, attractive and effective way for people to collect money.

A Justgiving account can also be used to:

• Raise money for charity by any sort of activity – shaving your head, a sponsored silence, stopping smoking, slimming, etc.

• Celebrate a birthday, wedding, anniversary or birth by raising money for a special cause.
• Create a memorial to someone by collecting money for a cause they favoured.

Running in a marathon

How do you go about being accepted to run in a marathon?
• You and any of your supporters can apply to run – your name will then go into a ballot, and you just hope that you are successful.
• Many charities are allocated entries by the organizers. If you would like to be allocated an entry, then contact the organizers. Runners who are unsuccessful in the main ballot system may then contact you and ask you for your allocated place which you will give them if they agree to raise money for you. Even if a runner does get a place through the ballot, they may not know which charity to support; they may look at those charities with allocated places and approach one they are particularly interested in supporting.

Raising sponsorship

There are two main ways of raising sponsorship:
• The runners ask their friends and colleagues. They can set themselves a target for the amount they will raise, or the charity they are running for can agree this with them.
• The charity can ask its supporters to sponsor the runner and make this into a major fundraising promotion.

The sponsorship amount that you request can be based either on the number of miles or kilometres the runner completes, the time taken to complete the course, or a fixed amount as a donation (whether or not the runner completes the course or how long it takes).

Do this

After organizing an event, make sure you hold a debriefing session to establish what went well and what needs improving. Also try to get feedback from participants as to how the event went from their point of view (asking their friends for money and participation in the event itself).

Street parties, fairs and village fêtes

A street party is a great fundraising idea for a neighbourhood group. You can celebrate all that's good in the neighbourhood, bring everyone together for a bit of fun and raise lots of money. A summer fair or village fête is similar, but will be held in a park or a playground or on a village green.

To make it work, you will need:

• Plenty of time to plan the event and an active and committed group of people running it.
• Lots of stalls with fun things to do (fairground and party games from coconut shies and tug-of-wars to face painting), interesting things to buy (crafts, home-cooked food, etc.) good music and a great atmosphere.
• A celebrity to open the event, if possible, to attract participants and publicity.
• Lots of people coming along and spending lots of money (you can charge an admission fee as well as charging people for everything they do or buy).
• A well-designed poster or flyer that you can stick up everywhere and put through people's letterboxes.
• Some advance publicity in your local paper.
• Good weather – you may or may not be lucky with the weather, so if a washout will mean financial disaster you should consider insuring against bad weather (see box opposite).

Re-inventing the village fête at the V & A

Every year the Victoria & Albert Museum in London hosts a fête at which artists and designers are invited to create their own very special stall and try to raise as much money as they can.

These are some of the stalls that featured in the 2005 fair:

• Bubble-gum blowing – blow the biggest bubble and be filmed while you do it.

• Bubble-wrap mow down – just like a tug-of-war, only the two competitors race to pop all the bubbles on their side of a strip of bubble wrap.

• Lucky dip nail bar – put your hands through two holes in a screen, and two nail artists paint your nails using both colour and humour.

• Bounce a ping-pong ball into a ceramic urinal – three are placed at different levels. Marcel Duchamp once exhibited a urinal as a 'Ready-Made' work of art.

• Make your own geodesic dome – using an office stapler and thirty postcards.

• Flyaway paper planes – build your own aeroplane and see how far you can get it to go with an elastic catapult.

The V & A village fête is organized by Scarlet Projects: www.scarletprojects.com.

Greetings cards

Around ten per cent of all Christmas cards sent are charity cards. These may be produced and sold by a charity (either directly or in partnership with a greetings card manufacturer) or sold by a retailer with a small percentage of the sales price donated to a charity. Before deciding to produce your own charity cards, consider the following:

• Can you sell the cards you produce?

• Do you have enough supporters who might be interested in buying cards?

• Do you have volunteers to run a market stall?

• Are you organizing a big event in early December?

Must know

Weather insurance

A number of specialist insurance companies offer insurance against bad weather. However, you must examine the conditions that need to be satisfied for claims to be made. There would be nothing worse than taking out an expensive policy, then having to cancel your event only to find that you do not qualify for a payout. Typically, you have to pay around £500 for £10,000 of cover, but it could be worth it. Check out:

• Insurex Expo-Sure: www.insurex-exposure.com

• Weather Risk Marketing: www.wrm.co.uk

• Event Insurance Services: www.events-insurance.co.uk

• Weather Direct: www.weatherdirect.co.uk

5 Raising money through fundraising activities

Did you know?

Charity Projects

Charity Projects was set up by Jane Tewson in the 1980s to raise money for charity. One of its first events was the Nether Wallop Festival. This was just an ordinary village fête, but unbeknown to the locals, many celebrities from the world of entertainment came along and the whole event was filmed for television. Shortly afterwards, Charity Projects went on to create Comic Relief, which raises money through its Red Nose Day telethon, which is held once every two years.

Producing greetings cards

If you decide to go ahead, here are some ways of doing it:

• Design and produce your own cards entirely by hand (perhaps even using hand-made card). This is hard work, and means that you could only produce a few.

• Produce the cards on your computer. Again this is a good option if you just want to produce a few.

• Go to a High Street print shop. Many now have a selection of cards that can be over-printed with your organization's details.

• If you intend to produce 5,000 or more cards (equivalent to 500 packs of ten), you could approach Card Aid (see page 123) who print cards for a range of charities.

Having chosen your production method, you need to decide on the card design, size and price.

The cards' design should reflect the spirit of Christmas but also convey something of the values of your organization – for example, a secular or multi-faith charity might want a card with a message of peace rather than a picture of the Virgin Mary.

Size and price will be linked and it is important, in this respect, to know your market. While large businesses and more wealthy people will buy larger, more expensive cards, people who are less well off will buy special-offer boxes of cards that are sold far cheaper than you could ever produce on your own. For a smaller organization, a medium-size card is a good option.

A good ploy for making more money is to pack the cards in fives or eights, rather than in tens – you will find that people's purchasing decisions are very much influenced by the headline price rather than the cost per card.

Charity shops

Charity shops are usually found in towns or cities and often in prime high-street locations. They sell donated goods – either second-hand or ends of lines donated by manufacturers – to raise funds for a charity. As well as raising money, they give the charity in question a high-street presence, thereby increasing public awareness, and they provide a source of cheap clothing and household items for people on low incomes.

Around 6,500 charity shops throughout the UK today raise more than £90 million each year. Most sell clothing, books, toys, ornaments, kitchenware, videos, music, computer games, furnishings and bric-a-brac. Some also sell furniture and electrical appliances (care needs to be taken to ensure that safety standards are adhered to), and some are specialist shops selling such things as books and bridal wear.

More than ninety per cent of the goods sold in charity shops are donated. Some shops supplement their stock with bought-in goods including gifts, cards, calendars and stationery that are sold through their Christmas catalogue, promotional items such as mugs and t-shirts, books and ethically-produced or fairly-traded goods.

Before deciding to run a charity shop, consider these issues:
• Is a suitable shop available? And is it in a good enough location?
• Can you afford the cost of the shop? You may have to pay a rent or a service charge; you will have to pay twenty per cent business rates (the remaining eighty per cent is a tax concession given to charity shops selling mainly donated goods, although your local authority does have the power to waive the twenty per cent); and you might need to do some repairs and redecorations.

Want to know more?

Charity cards

The following schemes are run either by a charity or co-operatively for charities:
• Cards for Good Causes: www.cardsforcharity.co.uk
• Card Aid: www.cardaid.co.uk
• Combined Charities Christmas Shops: www.christmas-cards.org.uk

Think about this

You can generate some income for your organization by selling Christmas cards and this will spread awareness of your charity and the work it is doing. However, the income can be hard-earned, as the cards have to be designed, printed and sold and there is always a risk that you will be left with unsold stock, leaving you out of pocket.

• Are there lots of other charity shops near by? If so, how will yours be distinctive? (You could specialize in specific merchandise, perhaps.)
• Is there someone who is prepared to be responsible for managing the shop and seeing that it is run properly and successfully?
• Do you have enough willing volunteers to collect donated goods and to serve in the shop?

How to run a charity shop

Having acquired a shop you will then need to:
• Organize house-to-house collections.
• Price the goods.
• Ensure that all your stock is clean and effectively displayed.
• Adopt a procedure for disposing of (recycling) goods you don't want.
• Train your volunteers to be friendly, helpful and polite.

If something particularly valuable turns up, you could auction it on eBay. You could get additional publicity by donating surplus clothes to a homeless day centre or by organizing a fashion show as a fundraising event. Or you could fill up bags or shoe boxes with miscellaneous household items which you then sell sight unseen for £5 as a 'lucky dip'.

As an alternative to running a charity shop, you might consider collecting goods and then selling them at car boot sales to raise money for your organization. Or, if you have enough storage space, you might organize a once-a-year jumble sale.

The advantage of both of these options is that there is no up-front investment in a building nor is there the need for volunteers. You can just do it when you want and when you have lots to sell.

Selling information and expertise

Your expertise or other information can help you to generate funds for your organization.

• **Publications.** These can help you to promote an idea or a way of working. If your publication is really needed, people will be prepared to pay for it.

Chiswick Women's Aid, for example, was the first ever refuge for abused women, and to provide information and advice for social workers CWA produced and sold *Battered Women and the Law*. Changemakers, on the other hand, received a grant from the Department for Education and Science to document its working practices in a manual entitled *Enhancing the Enterprise Skills in Young People*. The DfES distributed copies of this manual for free and the funds in this instance were raised from the sponsor for producing the publication, rather than from sales income.

• **Training.** This is another way of earning money from your expertise. It requires an expert (who should have reasonable training or facilitation skills), a training room and participants. Commercial training providers charge many hundreds of pounds a day for participation. You may want to charge something more affordable. You may have a particular expertise that will be the centrepiece of the training.

As an example, Directory of Social Change, which provides training and information for charities, brought an expert on Japanese corporate philanthropy to the UK to run a two-day workshop for major arts and educational institutions.

• **Conferences**. For a conference, you could select a burning current issue for discussion, assemble a programme of high-powered authoritative speakers, produce a brochure and find or rent suitable mailing lists to promote the event. You will book an impressive venue (the catering is likely to be more expensive than the booking charge), ask someone well known

> **Want to know more?**
>
> **Charity shops**
>
> Contact the Association of Charity Shops: www.charityshops.org.uk

Did you know?

The website www.lulu.com enables you to upload the text and illustrations for your publication, design the pages and the cover, print only as many copies as you need (even just one) and sell the publication in hard copy or electronic form from the website.

to chair the proceedings and do all you can to make it a success.

• **Contracts for services.** Many organizations sell their services either to the end-user, or to their local authority or the NHS. Contract income for providing services is now an important way of generating funds, especially in the field of social and health care, although how to go about doing it is something that falls beyond the scope of this book.

How to charge

If you produce publications or organize training or conferences, first define your objectives. Are you doing it primarily to get across information or to generate money? Or is it a mixture of the two? Your objectives will determine your charging structure.

Be aware of your market. If you are planning a workshop for unemployed people or for self-help groups working with no resources you will want to make the participation fee nominal. But if you are dealing with people who can pay, then charge what you think is appropriate (based on the value of attending, their ability to pay and your own financial objectives). You might charge a differential rate for members, for community organizations and for people from the public or commercial sectors.

Remember to build in a budget line for promotion.

Getting people to advertise in your publications

Your publications provide you with a great opportunity to generate money through sponsorship or advertising. Sponsorship is where someone pays either all the costs (or a substantial part) of producing and distributing your publication in return for being acknowledged as 'sponsor'. They might be a company wanting to be associated with your organization or a government agency wanting to disseminate a particular message. Think about who might be interested in sponsoring you and how they might benefit. Then try to meet up with them for a preliminary discussion.

Advertising, on the other hand, takes one of two forms:

• **Goodwill advertising** – where the advertising pays for a public acknowledgement without any real expectation of a commercial return.

• **Commercial advertising** – where the advertiser hopes to reach potential customers who might be interested in their products or services.

Advertising can appear in your newsletters, annual reports, one-off publications, programmes for fundraising events, posters, calendars, wall charts and so on. Any advertising you take should be compatible with your organization's values, so if you are addressing health issues it would be inappropriate to promote junk food. You must also ensure that the character of your publication is not diminished by having advertisements – use them to enhance it with useful information and by breaking up the text on the page.

If you are going to solicit advertising you should:

• Think about who might be interested – your supporters (as a goodwill gesture), local businesses (to support something that's locally important as well as to promote their products or services), local government (to disseminate local information).

• Calculate the rates you will charge and produce a Rate Card (see box on page 128)

• Persuade anyone who might be interested; for small businesses, it is helpful to offer to design their advertisement.

Next, send advertisers a proof copy of their advertisement so that they can check for mistakes. Finally, send them a copy of the publication in which their advertisement is printed.

Do this

Do all you can to make sure that what you put on or publish achieves a high level of excellence. If it's worth doing, it's worth doing well.

Must know

Rates

A Rate Card sets out the cost of advertisements, taking into account different sizes, colour and position. The information on your Rate Card will include:
• Page size and the dimensions of different-sized advertisements.
• Print run and details of distribution.
• Colour availability.
• Rates.
• Deadline for agreeing to take space.
• Deadline for receiving artwork.
• Payment details.
• Your contact details.

Getting people to advertise on your website

Advertising and sponsorship can also be used to generate income via your website.

Sponsorship

You may be able to find a sponsor for your website. For example, the Refuge (Women's Aid) website is sponsored by the Body Shop, which enhances the company's ethical credentials and associates it with a cause to which they are sympathetic.

To get a company to sponsor your website, you will need evidence of the numbers (and if possible, the type of people) using your website. You can then link the advertiser's target audience with the type of people who visit your website. Things like location, buying habits, interests, age and gender are also important factors when seeking sponsorship, and you can get these from a user survey.

In return for sponsorship you could offer a banner advertisement on your homepage and a notice stating that 'This website is sponsored by ...', with a link to the sponsor's homepage.

Advertising

Advertising can be included on your homepage (or any other frequently visited page), usually in the form of a 'banner advertisement' across the top or a 'tower block advertisement' on the side. You could also try a patchwork quilt, where each advertiser gets a small square and clicking on that square takes the user to the relevant homepage. (See the Million Dollar Homepage described in the box opposite.)

Selling books and CDs from your website

You can use your website to sell books and CDs – whether your own or other titles selected by you. This can be a useful service for website visitors, as well as a source of money for you. And if you don't want the bother of handling orders, posting them out and collecting the cash, you can become an Amazon Associate: this means that the sales are made from Amazon's website and you are paid a small percentage (between four and ten per cent) for the sales that your website generates. If orders grow, you might then consider whether you want to start handling the orders yourself (see right for how to apply).

There are also services on the Internet that enable you to publish your own books, CDs and DVDs electronically and sell them from your website. The products are either downloadable (in which case you receive a royalty), or can be printed on demand and sent to purchasers. The website pioneering this is www.lulu.com (see box on page 126). You may find that this will transform your production of information and at the same time generate some income for you.

Want to know more?

• A Leicester student raised nearly one million dollars by selling 'pixels' at $1 each in units of 10 x 10 ($100 per unit). See the result on Million Dollar Homepage (www.milliondollarhome page.com).
• Or take a look at 365 Ways to Change the World (www.365act. com) for another example of this.
• You can also use Google AdSense, where your site is linked to relevant advertisers, and you are paid per click. Find out more from: www.google.com/ adsense.
• To become an Amazon Associate, go to: http:// associates.amazon.co.uk /gp/ associates/join/ main.html.

6 Support in kind

Securing a gift in kind can be a really good first
step in forming a relationship with a supporter.
Your aim is to make them enthusiastic about
your work and proud that they are helping you
to the extent that they will eventually support
you on a regular basis – with products, services,
advice and even cash.

Identifying supporters

Your first step is to identify companies and individuals who might have what you need. You can ask your colleagues or friends for suggestions or do some simple research, using business directories or going through business networks such as the local Chamber of Commerce.

Do this

It is important to treat your gift-in-kind donors just as you would any other donor, so always remember to thank them and to keep in regular contact with them.

Getting support in kind

For things such as used office equipment, it's best to approach larger companies, as they are more likely to replace their equipment on a regular basis. For donations of products, you might approach the manufacturer, the wholesaler or a retail outlet. As a rule of thumb, the further back in the chain you go, the less it will cost them to donate it to you.

Usually, the higher up in the company the person you are approaching is, the better. But remember, there is also a 'back door'. For example, if you are looking for wood offcuts from a timber supplier you could formally ask the Managing Director (front door); or you could ask the Yard Manager to let you take some wood away (back door). Either way, the point is to ask someone who is able to make the decision – whoever that person is.

Once you know whom you are going to ask, it is far better to contact them in person or by telephone (unsolicited letters are often either ignored or thrown away). That way you are more likely to get an immediate decision. If you telephone and they ask you to write in, then do so, but remember to follow up with a phone call a few days later. You may need to be persistent to be successful. When you ask, remember to do the following:
• State your request, giving good reasons why you need the gift in question and explaining how important it is for your work.

Tell them that you expect to get a lot of good publicity and that you will ensure that people get to hear about their generosity. You can also point out that a gift in kind is a much cheaper and easier option than a donation.

• Be positive and enthusiastic – a good telephone manner is really important, so if that's not your strong point ask somebody else to do it.

• Have a fallback position in case your would-be donor says 'No'. For example, you might say '... but if you have last season's model, or damaged goods that would be fine for us.' Or '... if you can't donate it, would you consider giving us a discount – say fifty per cent?' Or 'I'm really sorry you can't help us, but do you know anyone who could?' You could then telephone that person saying you are ringing at so-and-so's suggestion.

What can be donated as a gift in kind?

• **Used equipment** – such as a computer, fax machine or office furniture. Many companies replace their equipment quite regularly and would prefer to find a good use for it than to throw it away. Similarly, your friends or supporters may be upgrading their equipment.

• **Use of equipment** – photocopying equipment to produce a large report or video-conferencing facilities for an important meeting. Any costs involved (such as paper or telephone calls) are usually not noticed.

• **Company facilities** – you can ask for a boardroom for an important meeting, or a training centre for a workshop.

• **Services** – advertising and PR agencies (for promotion), accountants (for tax and bookkeeping), management consultants (for drawing up a business plan), lawyers (for legal advice), architects and surveyors (for anything to do with

Did you know?

Comic Relief

When Comic Relief's Red Nose Day first started, they had a policy of getting everything they needed donated. For example, Marks & Spencer donated vouchers that were used to buy sandwiches and juices for lunch meetings and five local companies were persuaded to put Comic Relief's mail through their franking machines, each of the five taking one day a week.

buildings), etc. This sort of help is normally given in a voluntary capacity and out of office hours, although some large companies do allow time for employees to help in the community. Alternatively, you could approach an individual, and ask them to help you in a personal capacity.

• **Raw materials** – such as offcuts that would otherwise be thrown away.

Getting your costs sponsored

You are organizing an event and you want to get all the main costs covered. A good way of doing this is to make a 'shopping list' of all the different things you will be spending money on, and to ask people either to donate them or to cover their costs by sponsoring them.

Step 1: Make a list of all the items you need. This is your shopping list. It is similar to a wish list, but with one important difference: you are using it to raise cash as well as gifts in kind.

Step 2: Put a cost next to each item. This need not be the exact cost of paying for the item, as it can include an allowance for your administrative overheads and the costs of organizing the event (a rough rule of thumb is to double up on the actual cost). Where there are particularly attractive items on your shopping list, increase the amount you are asking for as people will be prepared to pay a bit more.

Step 3: Approach companies and individuals. Ask them either to donate an item or to sponsor it.

While trying to get each of the items on your list paid for, you could also try to find an 'event sponsor' who would pay for all the bigger items in return for being acknowledged as the event's main sponsor. They might even pay for t-shirts for all the volunteers who will be helping out on the day. But remember to tell them that this is an added benefit for which they will have to pay.

Your job is to 'sell' everything on your list. Remember that your fundraising objectives are to cover the cost of the event by paying for everything you need and also to raise something towards your administration costs.

Try to look at things from the point of view of the person you are approaching. Will they view you as a nuisance? Or will they actually be interested in hearing about your work and being given the opportunity to support you? Whatever you do, don't be a bore.

Want to know more?

• **Use trade directories, Yellow Pages or your business phone book to identify companies in your area who might be persuaded to help.**
• **To target national companies, visit their website (Google will help you find it) and approach their head office.**
• **See chapter 7 for advice on getting support from large organizations.**

7 Getting support from trusts, companies and governments

There's a lot of money out there just waiting to be awarded to deserving causes. Here's how to apply and convince the powers that be that your charity is worthy of their support.

How to make an approach

The right approach makes all the difference. In this chapter, you'll learn how to approach big organizations and apply for grants from them.

Must know

Cuttings file

Keep copies of every article about your organization and anything relating to the issue you are addressing. Seeing this kind of evidence of your track record may help to influence those who are in a position to help you.

Support from grant-making trusts

Grant-making trusts – sometimes referred to as 'foundations' – are charities whose purpose is to give money to charity. In the UK, they give away around £2 billion a year. Trusts come in many and varied forms, but have the following in common:

• Their main purpose is to give grants. They have a specific annual budget to this end and would-be beneficiaries compete for the available funds.

• They give money for charitable purposes. They nearly always require that you are registered as a charity, although it may be possible to find another charity to receive the grant on your behalf, and then pass it on to you for your charitable work.

• They are private organizations controlled by a Board of Trustees, which sets the policy and guidelines for applications and decides who to support. The trust's constitution will define the Objects (which set out *how* the money can be spent) and the Beneficial Area (which sets out *where* the money can be spent). Some trusts are very tightly constrained by their constitution; others are able to spend what they like, where they like. However, even where their constitution allows them to spend their money how they like, they may decide to restrict their grant-making by having a grants policy.

Different sorts of trusts

• Local or national: some trusts are very local, confining their grant-making to a particular town or parish. For example, the Cripplegate Foundation spends its money in the Cripplegate area bordering the City of London. The Wates Foundation has a particular interest in supporting projects in south London.

There is a group of trusts known as 'community foundations' whose purpose it is to give money in a defined community. They also raise capital and income towards their grant-making budget. The community foundation serving Tyne & Wear and Northumberland and the Greater Bristol Foundation are examples of these.

• **General or specialist**: some trusts devote their grant-making to a specified purpose. For example, the UK's biggest trust is the Wellcome Trust (which used to own the Wellcome pharmaceutical company, now absorbed into GlaxoSmithKline), which makes all its grants for the advancement of health and research resources in medical history. The Tudor Trust and the Esmee Fairbairn Foundation have more general purposes, although they define priority areas for support, which are revised from time to time.

• **Endowed**: most trusts will have some sort of endowment – shares or property that they own – which generates an annual income. Others, like Comic Relief and BBC Children in Need, will do their own fundraising to generate the income they give away.

• **Private or public**: although trusts are independent bodies set up to make grants for public benefit, some are controlled by a founder or a family

Think about this

Trusts receive far too many applications, but far too few really good ones. A good application is not only a well-written one, but one that relates to a project with a spark of originality and excitement, submitted by an organization that can show that it is capable of doing what it promises.

and only make grants to projects known to them or which they personally decide to support.

• **Old or new:** some charities were established centuries ago whereas others are very new. The older ones may have more old-fashioned purposes. For example the Metropolitan Drinking Fountain and Cattle Trough Association can only use its money to put up drinking fountains and cattle troughs in London. It now provides small grants for drinking fountains in school playgrounds and public places but the need today for cattle troughs is obviously redundant. A charity set up now would have today's needs in mind.

• **Large or small:** some trusts give away huge amounts of money and make large grants; others are tiny, making very small grants or providing Christmas hampers to pensioners in a particular area.

Why approach a trust?

You should consider approaching a trust for the following reasons:

• They have a total estimated annual giveaway of £2 billion for charitable purposes.

• Each has its own policy and priorities so you should be able to find at least one that would be interested in what you are doing.

• On the whole, they prefer to fund projects that are not receiving Government funding, they like innovation (new ideas for tackling problems or addressing newly emerging problems) and they are often prepared to take more risks.

• The application process is quite simple. They do not require a huge amount of information and they make their decisions relatively quickly.

Which type of trust should you approach?

The answer to this is that you should be approaching any that are most likely to be interested in what you are doing.

National trusts support mainly two things: national initiatives and local initiatives that are of wider interest (on the basis that what you are doing is innovative in some way, and if you succeed it may be replicable elsewhere).

Local trusts may be interested in supporting you if what you are doing brings local benefit, so find out who they are. Some national trusts also make local grants in particular areas – perhaps in the locality in which they are based, or in an area of high deprivation where few trusts are active or because of some historical connection.

If you are working with young people there could be interest from both national and local trusts. Your job is to find those trusts with a stated interest in supporting your area of work, and then to persuade them that yours is one of the best projects around.

Smaller trusts will make small grants, so if you are looking for £10,000 or more, there will be no point approaching a trust with an annual income of less than £100,000. They would be unlikely to support you at the level you need, because this would represent too high a proportion of their annual grants budget.

If you have had a grant from a particular trust in the past it might be worth approaching that trust for further support. Equally if either you or your organization are known personally to any trust this can be useful. Do some research based on these criteria, then draw up a 'hit list' of those trusts you will apply to.

The trusts on the following pages are all members of the Association of Charitable Foundations. The way in which each of them approaches the business of grant-making clearly illustrates the diversity of trusts.

The Baring Foundation

This trust makes £2.8 million of grants each year. In 2006, its arts programme supported organizations working with refugees and asylum seekers. It also makes largish grants to a few organizations that are seeking to strengthen the voluntary sector or that work in Sub-Saharan Africa. The Baring family are closely associated with the foundation.

This trust has a very specific programme. If your work fits within its current policy, then your best bet is to contact them with an outline of what you are planning before submitting a formal application.

The Barrow Cadbury Trust

Set up in 1920 as the Barrow & Geraldine S. Cadbury Trust, it merged with the Paul S. Cadbury Trust. Its aim is to promote a fair, equal, peaceful and democratic society and it works alongside the Barrow Cadbury Fund, which supports non-charitable initiatives with a similar purpose. The trust supports bridge-building between policy makers and the grassroots, seeks to identify best practice from projects that promote social change and encourages new solutions to old problems. It has an annual grants budget of £3.2 million and its average grant is just over £30,000. This trust has a long tradition of supporting social justice from a Quaker perspective. If you have a great idea, they could be interested.

The annual BBC Children in Need appeal

Around £35 million is raised to support children-in-need projects across the UK. In 2004–05 the appeal made 1,754 grants totalling just over £34.4 million with an average grant of £2,000. Applicants need to be working with disadvantaged children under eighteen and should show how their work improves children's lives. 'Disadvantaged' can include any kind of disability, behavioural or psychological problems, living in poverty, deprivation, illness, distress, abuse or neglect. Children in Need funds are contributed by donors from all around the UK, and the trust spreads its money widely. If you are doing work that fits its guidelines it is worth applying. You would stand a reasonable chance.

Bridge House Trust

Part of the Corporation of London, this trust makes grants of £17 million a year for the benefit of the inhabitants of Greater London. The trust's original purpose was to maintain London Bridge. Over the centuries it acquired property assets both in the City and the surrounding countryside and in the nineteenth century built Blackfriars Bridge, purchased Southwark Bridge and constructed Tower Bridge. In February 2002, the trust took over ownership and maintenance of the pedestrian-only Millennium Bridge. In 1995, it had its powers widened to make grants. It now supports access for disabled people, London's environment, children and young people, older people in the community and strengthening London's voluntary and community sectors. Alongside this it has been running a small grants programme. Bridge House is one of two major London-based trusts, the other being City Parochial Foundation. You should apply if you are running an interesting project in London within its area of focus.

The Worshipful Company of Butchers

This has a general charity, making fifty grants of an average of £500 each year to London-based charities. It supports the education and training of persons engaged or about to be engaged in the meat processing industry in the UK, and promotes research into the science of meat processing techniques. Assuming that you are not engaged in meat processing, then you are unlikely to get support unless you have some personal contact with the Livery Company.

Must know

Be brief

Most trusts complain about the excessive length of the applications they receive. Make it easy for them by keeping it as short as possible, while at the same time providing them with all the information they need to make a decision.

Applying to trusts

A good starting point for finding the right trusts to approach is to look at the annual reports of charities similar to yours, as the grants they have received may be listed in their accounts. You can also ask around to see if anyone can suggest possible funders.

Another starting point is a directory – use one of the published directories of grant-making trusts:
• *The Guide to the Major Trusts*, published in several volumes by the Directory of Social Change.
• *The Directory of Grant Making Trusts*, published by the Charities Aid Foundation and distributed by Directory of Social Change.

'FunderFinder' and 'Trust Funding' develop and distribute software that enables you to search for trusts and foundations to match your organization's profile and that of the project requiring funding. You key in a number of criteria, and the search then comes up with a list of likely funders. You will then need to research the entries on this list further.

If you are a local organization, Directory of Social Change publishes a number of guides to local trusts and your local Council of Voluntary Service may maintain a database of local trusts or have a range of up-to-date trust directories that you can consult. They may also give you access to 'FunderFinder' or 'Trust Funding' software.

Researching would-be funders

If you are approaching a larger trust it is worth finding out a bit more about them:
• Go to the trust's website. Many larger trusts now have a website explaining their policies and application procedures. The Association of Charitable Foundations provides links to the websites of its members: www.acf.org.uk/linkstrusts.htm.

• Telephone for a copy of the trust's guidelines for applicants or annual report (if you can't get what you need from its website).

• Talk to people doing similar work to see who is supporting them and to ask for their ideas and advice.

When doing your research, think carefully about the following:

• Do you fit within the trust's geographical criteria?

• Do you fit within its policy and priority areas of grant-making?

• What size grants does the trust normally make, and how does this relate to your needs? You may find that the trust makes some larger grants, some smaller grants and even some very small local grants. If you have never had a grant from them before, you are unlikely to receive a large one. They will want to support something smaller and see how it goes before committing a larger sum of money.

• What is it about your work that might appeal to the trust?

There is a lot of information available on trusts. But the information available to you is also available to everybody else. What would be really nice would be to find a large trust that is not listed in any directory and which appears to be interested in supporting just what you are doing! These do exist. Not all trusts are documented and new ones are formed every year. Do some detective work: follow up rumours and find out what you can from the Charity Commission register or GuideStar.

Want to know more?

• Contact your local Council of Voluntary Service. You can get contact details from www.navca.org.uk
• Contact Directory of Social Change at www.dsc.org.uk

How to apply

Step 1: Find out as much as you can about the trust. Use this information to tailor your application to the trust, ensuring that what you are proposing is something that you want to do and not just something that they might pay for. If you have had any previous contact with the trust it is helpful as you will not then be applying 'out of the blue'.

Step 2: Check whether there is an official application form or whether you are simply required to send a letter. Find out about the decision-making cycle. Larger trusts may meet quarterly or even monthly to decide on applications; some smaller trusts might respond to an application on receipt, or make all their decisions each year in a single day. You can do all of this by visiting their website or be telephoning their offices.

Step 3: Assemble all the information you will need. This includes deciding your budget. At this stage it can be helpful to arrange a preliminary meeting with the trust or to invite them to visit you and meet some of the beneficiaries.

Step 4: Complete your application (see 'Writing an application', page 175). Make sure you answer all the questions, emphasizing those factors that are likely to convince them to support you. If you are unknown to them, you might want to provide some endorsements alongside your application.
If the trust doesn't say how it likes people to apply, a short covering letter (no more than a page) summarizing your proposal and highlighting some of the key points (backed up by enclosures of more detailed plans, budgets and other supporting information) usually works well.

Step 5: Send off your application before the deadline. It is sometimes a good idea to telephone to check that it has arrived.

Step 6: Wait. Some trusts might want to meet with you or even visit you as part of their assessment process; other than this there is little more you can do, except wait for their decision.

Making decisions
• Many small trusts and some family trusts are administered by one of the trustees, often from their home.

• Some smaller trusts use an accountant or a solicitor to act as correspondent for receiving applications, which are then passed on to the trustees. Some might appoint a part-time administrative secretary.

• Larger trusts may have a full-time grants secretary to assess applications, meet applicants and make recommendations to the trustees.

• The very large trusts will have a professionally-staffed office dealing with applications under a trust director who reports to the trustees.

Where professional staff are employed they sometimes have the discretion to make grants up to a certain level without taking the application to the trustees. For very large trusts, the limit can be as high as £20,000.

Getting support from companies

The top 500 UK companies give around £300 million each year, plus considerable support in kind. In terms of money, companies are not that important a source of funding, but the wide range of things they can provide makes them attractive to fundraisers.

The main function of any company is to do business and make a profit. They need good reasons for giving away some of their profits and it is important to understand these reasons before you approach them. This will help you to find the right companies and to frame your application appropriately.

Companies give money to charity:

• To be associated with certain causes – mining and extraction companies support environmental projects, for example, pharmaceutical companies support health projects, banks support economic development projects, and so on; this enhances their image, but also gives them a different perspective and good contacts on a social issue that is important to them.

Must know

Take note

Companies are unlikely to support:
• Local appeals where they have no business presence.
• Religious appeals, although they may support social and community projects run by religious bodies.
• Circular appeals.
• Controversial causes.

• To create goodwill – they want to be well thought of within the communities in which they operate and as a caring company by society at large; they are expected to support local projects.
• To create goodwill amongst their employees, who will think more favourably of them as a result of the worthwhile work they support.
• Because they are asked to – and it is expected; no company wants to be thought of as mean.
• Because of a special interest – if the chairman or a senior director favours a particular cause or organization, they may find a way for the company to support it.
• Because an employee is involved – many companies encourage employee involvement as they believe it helps them to do their jobs better (for example by developing leadership, communication skills and creativity).
• To generate good publicity both for their products and for their 'corporate image' – so if you can deliver good publicity in return for their support they will be more likely to want to support you.
• To provide entertainment opportunities – companies like to sponsor prestigious entertainment, cultural and sporting events, say at the Royal Opera House or a major art exhibition at the Tate Modern or the FA Cup final, to which they can invite their important customers and suppliers.
• For tax relief benefits – these are an added bonus but seldom the determining factor.

Some useful points to remember
• Companies are usually only interested in local projects in areas where they have a business presence.
• If a member of the company's staff is involved in your work in some way this can encourage the company to give.

• It is shareholders' funds that are being given away, so public companies will always need a good reason for giving support. Most do give something although there are a very few that will say it is not their job to support charity and to use shareholders' funds for non-business related purposes.

• There may be more money in the marketing budget or the human resources budget than in the charity budget – if you approach the person responsible for these you might be able to persuade them that spending money on your scheme is an effective use for their funds.

• Companies like to give efficiently – they will look for ways of giving at little cost or getting a good return (in PR or other terms).

There are all sorts of ways of identifying the right companies.

Make use of existing contacts

Do an audit of contacts – find out who in your organization (your Board, your staff, your volunteers) knows whom. If this throws up people you might want to approach, discuss with that person how best to approach their contact. If a volunteer or board member works for a company, get them to request support from their employer.

Use local knowledge

Get to know the local business scene. Take a walk around town, go and see local trading estates, read the local newspaper to see who's doing well and so on.

Use directories

Use the online and published directories of company giving. Use trade directories, which list companies in particular industries

Must know

Pound for pound

To encourage employee involvement in charities some larger companies have matched giving schemes where they give, pound for pound (or on some other formula), money raised or time given by an employee (see also page 154).

and sectors. Use Yellow Pages and other business telephone directories to identify local suppliers.

Make yourself known

Contact national business associations – some, such as the accountancy and surveying professions, have schemes for offering pro bono support to charities. Contact local business associations to ask if you could speak at a meeting.

What type of company gives?

Here are some of the different sorts of companies that might be interested in supporting you:

Leading national and multinational companies

These include banks, manufacturing companies, IT companies, shops and the service sector. Companies operating across the world often have a worldwide giving policy (this is true for most major US and UK companies). Sometimes the decisions will be made at international level and sometimes at national level.

In cases where a company has branches, they may make small local donations of cash, vouchers or gifts in kind via their stores at the discretion of the local manager. This happens, for example, with banks and supermarkets.

To get support from a leading company, you need to be:
• A national or nationally significant project.
• A local project working near the company's headquarters or a major business location.

Larger local companies

In any city or region there will be large companies that are important to the local economy. These companies will often feel a responsibility to do something to support community initiatives in their area. Some towns have one or more large companies based there who take an active role in supporting community projects, for example, Boots in Nottingham, Pilkington in St Helens and Zurich Financial Services in Swindon.

Branches and subsidiaries of large companies
A large company will have subsidiaries – such as Whitbread who owns Costa Coffee, TGI Fridays, Premier Inns and other brands. Some companies devolve their giving to subsidiaries. For others, it is centralized – although local branches might have the discretion to make very small grants.

Smaller local companies
There are always lots of smaller local companies – from those operating on trading estates, to the shops in the high street, to firms of professionals including solicitors, accountants and estate agents. These may well be interested in giving to local projects, advertising in a publication or supporting you in kind.

Who should you write to?
• The donations policy for larger companies will be agreed by the Board, and decisions on what to support will be made through a Community Affairs Department. They may publish their policy, procedures and guidelines in some sort of report. If you are looking for sponsorship, the Marketing Director or Brand Manager will be responsible for the marketing budget; or you might discuss your ideas first with the company's advertising agency.
• In medium-sized and smaller companies, it is usually the top person who will decide – the Chairman or the Managing Director – and it is important that you contact that person. It is worth telephoning their office first to check their name and job title before writing.

Must know

Newsletter

The Charities Information Bureau publishes a monthly funding newsletter that highlights new grants schemes by companies as well as other funders: www.cibfunding.org.uk.

What should you ask for?

There are many ways in which a company can contribute to your cause so you should consider what it is that you actually want from them. They might:

• Give you a cash donation, although most are unlikely to make large ones other than to a prestigious appeal or for a major project that they particularly want to support.

• Sponsor an event, activity or promotional and educational materials (see below).

• Give support in kind (see chapter 6) – because this is cheaper and easier than a donation it is often the best way of getting support from a company.

• Engage in a joint promotion (see page 154).

• Encourage employees to volunteer or become involved as a board member, by contributing a senior member of staff to serve in this capacity (see box page 154).

• Organize a fundraising campaign amongst employees – one method that is used in some countries is 'payroll giving' (see page 79).

• Lend you their board room or training facilities.

• Advertise in brochures and publications to get publicity and help defray the costs.

Business sponsorship

Broadly speaking, the difference between sponsorship and a donation is that a sponsor expects to receive some sort of benefit, whereas a donation is given to benefit the charity with the possible added bonus of some good publicity for the donor. The cost of the sponsorship will normally be paid for out of the promotions budget rather than the charity budget.

A local estate agent might, for example, sponsor a gymkhana as a way of reaching well-heeled families who are potential property buyers, while a leading accountancy firm could sponsor a world-class golf tournament, giving key clients the opportunity to play in a pro-am format with some of the world's leading golfers before the main event, and getting publicity for the company and its services. A national school debating competition might be sponsored by a newspaper so that it could promote itself to potential new readers and provide access to some of the country's leading young thinkers. And a bank could sponsor a financial literacy programme for secondary schools in order to introduce itself to young people who might become its customers.

How to get sponsorship

• Set out the benefits to the sponsor in a brief project proposal. Be as specific as you can. Don't just promise that they will get some 'good publicity'. Make a list of the coverage you expect to get for the event, and possibly even suggest a value for that.

• Approach the person who will make the decision. It can take time before anything is decided, and marketing budgets are often spent well ahead. So it is better to start looking for sponsors sooner rather than later. You can

Think about this

Consider the benefit to the sponsor and what this might be worth to them. You may be able to gain them access to things they could not get by themselves – for example, the chance to meet an A-list celebrity (which can then be reported in the company's in-house magazine) or access to young people in schools.

Case study

Bono has created a brand known as Product Red to raise money for fighting AIDS globally. There is a RED American Express card, a RED Motorola mobile phone, RED Converse shoes, a RED Gap t-shirt, and even RED Armani sunglasses (as worn by Bono). Money is donated to the Global Fund for AIDS for each product sold, and, in the case of the credit card and mobile phone, a proportion of the monthly customer spend.

Must know

Secondment of staff

Some companies will 'lend' you a member of their staff to work with you for free, either on an assignment to complete a job of work (such as to help you draw up a business plan) or to spend a longer period of time working with you full time (sometimes as an alternative to redundancy).

approach the company or its PR agency. If you have a great idea for a project, there are sponsorship consultants who might be interested in helping you to find a sponsor.

Joint promotions

A variation on the idea of sponsorship is what is called a 'joint promotion'. Here your organization teams up with a company to help sell its products or services.

Many charities market affinity credit cards to their supporters, receiving in return a fee for each new customer and a small percentage of the spend on the card. For the credit card company, this provides access to a mailing list of potential customers, with the added benefit that the charity is promoting the service to people who are interested in supporting it.

Another idea is to persuade a local restaurant to donate all the tips that it gets on one evening to a local charity, which will get it publicity in the local newspaper and bring in new customers.

Central government funding

Central government provides funding for voluntary organizations in three quite different ways.

1. Grant-in-aid to national and nationally significant initiatives made by different departments. Most government departments in the UK make grants. The Office of the Third Sector, for example, is responsible for volunteering and the voluntary sector, so it gives a large annual grant to the National Council for Voluntary Organizations to help it fulfil its role as the representative body for the voluntary. It supports Community Service Volunteers for its work in mobilizing volunteers and to run the Year of the Volunteer in 2005. It supports the Muslim Youth Helpline which reaches out to young Muslims. It supports YouthNet to maintain the Do-It national volunteering website.

Much of this is core funding to leading voluntary organizations operating within the area of interest of the government department. Sometimes the money is provided to enable the organization to achieve a specified objective. Most organizations will be supported over a long period, although a particular grant may run from year to year.

If you believe that the work you are doing is of national significance, then you might try to get a government grant. This will demonstrate your credentials to be at the 'top table' and it will also increase your opportunities for consulting with government.

First of all, you need to establish which government department has responsibility for what you are doing.

Where you operate is also important – arrangements for Scotland, Wales and Northern Ireland may be devolved to country level.

2. Funding lines for specific purposes. The government often makes funds available in response to a particular issue – to demonstrate that it cares and is proactive, but also to engage the voluntary sector in creating solutions.

Sometimes these funding lines are extremely large and run for many years – for example, Sure Start for supporting pre-school children and their young mothers, or the New Deal for getting disengaged young people into employment. Others are much smaller and run in the short term.

Some schemes are run directly by the government department; others are run by another agency – for example, Y-Speak, which supported youth consultation, was first run by the DfES, then contracted out to Changemakers and finally devolved to a more local level.

3. **Funding provided by non-departmental public bodies.** The government has established a large number of public bodies and agencies to be responsible for a particular area of work. Many of these bodies run grants programmes. They include:
• The Arts Council and the Regional Arts Boards – for supporting the arts, along with similar bodies for museums and libraries and for sport.
• English Heritage and the National Heritage Memorial Fund – for heritage preservation.
• The Countryside Agency, English Nature and the Forestry Commission – for rural matters.
• The Housing Corporation and Housing Action Trusts – for social housing.
• The Regional Development Agencies and the Coalfields Regeneration Trust – for economic regeneration.
• The National Youth Agency, Connect Youth International (British Council) and the Commonwealth Youth Exchange Council – for youth matters.
• The Learning and Skills Council, for training and employability.
• The Legal Services Commission – for legal services.
• The Prison Service, the Police Service, the Probation Service and the Youth Justice Board – for crime and disorder.

• The Commission for Racial Equality, Equal Opportunities Commission and Disability Rights Commission – for equal rights.
• The National Health Service Authorities and Trusts – for delivering health care.

Finding your way around government

The main government departments supporting voluntary organizations directly or make funding lines available to charities are:
• The Office of the Third Sector within the Cabinet Office (or OTS, responsible for charities, voluntary organizations and volunteering).
• The Department for Education and Skills (or DfES, responsible for education and training).
• The Department of Health (responsible for health and wellbeing).
• The Home Office (responsible for immigration and citizenship, and crime).
• The Department for Communities and Local Government (or DCLG, responsible for housing, planning, regeneration, neighbourhood renewal and social exclusion). The DCLG is also responsible for the Government Offices for the Regions. These co-ordinate and support the provision of services in the nine English regions from the main spending departments.

Other departments include: Department of Media Culture and Sport, Department for International Development (which supports overseas development and development education in the UK), Department for Trade and Industry, Department for Transport, Department for Environment, Food and Rural Affairs, Department of Work and Pensions, and even the Foreign Office and the Ministry of Defence.

The following are examples of the sorts of funding available at the time of writing.

Want to know more?

• For a more detailed explanation of the structure of government funding see: www.cibfunding.org.uk/fund/page31.htm and to be kept up to date with the latest funding schemes, subscribe to the CIB Funding Newsletter: www.cibfunding.org.uk.
• To find out what funds are available from the Office of the Third Sector, DfES, the Department of Health, the Home Office, the DCLG and the Government Offices of the Regions and their area-based initiatives and to receive alerts when new funding lines become available, subscribe free to: www.governmentfunding.org.uk.

Department of Health

General grants: the Section 64 General Scheme of Grants is the Department of Health's main source of funding to the voluntary and community sector in England. The scheme is designed to strengthen and further develop the partnership between government and the voluntary and community sector.

Opportunities for volunteering: this distributes approximately £6.9 million per year to 300 local health and social care projects in England to enable local organizations to involve volunteers in their work.

Government Office for London's area-based initiatives

Community Champions Fund: up to £2,000 to support the work of local people who can encourage others to get more involved in renewing their neighbourhoods.

Community Learning Chests: up to £5,000 to fund activities to develop the skills and knowledge of communities to enable them to participate in neighbourhood renewal at a local level.

Neighbourhood Community Learning Chests: up to £5,000, this is part of the Single Community Programme, and funds projects that will improve the quality of life in the eighty-eight most deprived areas of England.

Lobbying your Member of Parliament

There may be times when you need the support of your Member of Parliament as someone who can endorse or support what you are doing, ask a question in parliament to the relevant Minister, or give you advice.

Your MP can be approached in one of two ways. Arrange to meet at a 'surgery' in their constituency, which will usually be held on a Friday or at weekends; contact their constituency office to find out when. Or you can arrange to meet them in the House of Commons. (Telephone 020 7210 3000 to be put through to their office.)

Before meeting your MP you must:
• Do some background research about them, their interests and how they have voted.
• Decide what you want to talk about, the points you plan to raise, the questions you will ask and what, specifically, you want them to do.

Then, when you meet them:
• Be brief so that you can get your points across in the (possibly short) time allocated.
• Take supporting literature and give details of a contact person, in case they need to follow up.
• Make a written note of the discussion and the key points made.

The Compact

The relationship between government and the voluntary sector can be problematic:
• Charities are not supposed to get involved in party politics.
• Most organizations are set up to achieve their own objectives and not those of government. However, there is an inherent danger in accepting funding that you end up doing what the government wants simply because the money is there.
• Charitable money should not be used to pay for things that are the responsibility of government. This can be difficult if the government is not

Must know

How government works

To get government support, it helps if you know about how government works and about latest government policies. Here are some information sources that will help you:
• **About My Vote** is a service from the Electoral Commission that explains the structure of government and elections: www.about myvote.co.uk
• If you want to find out about your MP, what they are interested in and how they have voted on some key issues, use this free website: www.theywork foryou.com
• If you want to write to your MP, member of the European Parliament, Greater London Authority Member or Local Councillor, just type in your postcode, choose who you want to write to and this website will send your e-mail to them: www.writetothem.com

Must know

Local grants

Find out more about
how your local authority
makes grants from your
local Council of
Voluntary Service. Visit
www.nacvs.org.uk/cvs
dir for contact details.

meeting people's needs even where it has an
obligation to do so.
• Some organizations find it hard to criticize
government if they are accepting its money.
• Government grants are often quite large, and this
can create a dependency – and lead to problems
when the grant is not renewed.

The idea of a Compact between government and
the voluntary and community sector was developed
by the Labour party before it came into power in
1997 as a means of improving their relationship for
mutual advantage (see www.thecompact.org.uk).

Local government funding

It is the responsibility of local government to offer a wide range
of services for the benefit of the local community and to ensure
its wellbeing. To enable them to fulfil this role, they receive a
proportion of the Council Tax we all have to pay, as well as an
allocation from Business Rates plus an annual grant from
central government. There is further revenue from parking fees
and other charges they make for the services they provide.
If yours is a service that benefits local people – whether it is
organizing a neighbourhood festival, an after-school club
or activities for young people during the school holidays,
shopping for the housebound or turning derelict land into a
garden – you may be eligible for a grant from your local council.

How local government is organized

Local authorities are responsible for education, housing, social
services, libraries, leisure and recreation (including the youth
service), planning, transport planning and public transport,
highways (apart from roads operated by the Highways Agency),
the fire service, waste collection and disposal including
recycling, environmental health and tourism.

The structure of local government is quite complex. There are different levels, each with different responsibilities:

• **Regional authorities.** The Greater London Authority is elected to oversee London-wide matters; the other English regions do not have elected bodies.

• **Metropolitan Councils.** Most big cities have a Metropolitan Council (in London, the Borough Councils fulfil the same role). These bodies deliver all local services, although in some cases passenger transport, the fire service and waste disposal may be run jointly by several local authorities.

• **County and District Councils.** In other areas County Councils are responsible for most services and District Councils deal with planning and more local services. In some areas, these two levels are combined into Unitary Authorities. These local authorities are run by elected councils and led by the Leader of the Council. (The role of Mayor is a purely ceremonial one other than in London.)

The Council may operate via a number of committees, each responsible for a particular area and led by a Chair. Councillors are elected for four years, and the Council will hold elections either every four or two years.

The Council area is divided into wards, each ward being represented by a number of Councillors.

Most Councillors are affiliated to a national political party, and one party or a coalition of two parties will have a majority of councillors and control the Council. They may have a party 'caucus' to decide party policy on particular issues. The actual work is done by Council Officers under the direction of a Chief Executive and departmental Directors.

Want to know more?

• To find out about regional funding through the Government Offices for the Regions (in England), go to the national website and click on your region: www.gos.gov.uk/national or go to the website of the Department you are particularly interested in.

• Local organizations should contact their Council of Voluntary Service or Rural Community Council, as a source of local information and advice. Contact details are available on www.navca.org.uk for CVSs and www.acre.org.uk for RCCs.

Must know

Timing

Except in the case of very small grants, which may be available through a Community Chest, there will usually be an annual timetable for grant applications. You will need to apply in late summer for grants that are announced around the start of the following financial year (1 April), so begin planning your application sooner rather than later.

Grants from local authorities

Local councils may support local voluntary organizations through:

• Programme funding – whereby a voluntary organization may receive a grant or a contract or a payment for providing a specific service.
• A grants budget, distributed on an annual basis.
• A Community Chest, which makes very small grants.
• Charities that the Council administers – these funds may be amalgamated with the grants budget.
• The Mayor's Appeal, used for a different purpose each year.
• Discretionary Rate Relief – registered charities can claim eighty per cent rate relief on the premises they occupy (the remaining twenty per cent may be given on a discretionary basis by the local Council).

Applying for a local-authority grant

When you apply, keep the following in mind:

• **Who is responsible?** Find out which department of which local authority is responsible for what you are doing. A good first point of contact is the Council of Voluntary Service, which can advise on what's available and how to apply. It is best to discuss your proposal with the right Council department – try to meet both the officers and the Chair of the relevant Committee.
• **The level of public benefit.** You must demonstrate the number of people you will be helping, the level of service you plan to provide and that you will be able to do all this in a cost-effective way.
• **Your project.** You must assess the degree of local need in terms of what your project is offering and this may vary across the Council area. It can be important to show that the level of unmet need in your area is particularly great, that what you

propose will not be duplicating an existing service or that you will be meeting a certain need in a more effective way than is currently being achieved.

• **Lobbying.** It helps if you rally political support where you can. It is especially important to get the active support of your local Ward Councillors so that they can lobby their colleagues.

• **Research policy and priorities.** Find out what you can about Council policy (look at published strategy papers and statements made by leading councillors, the majority party's manifesto, minutes of Council and Committee meetings and so on), ensuring that what you are proposing fits in with it. This provides a really good starting point for your application.

• **Community support.** Showing that you have community support is always an important consideration for a democratically elected body.

Case study

The London Borough of Camden makes grants totalling £7.5 million to 115 local organizations. These include community centres, arts organizations, nurseries, play and youth centres, advice agencies and training providers. Grants are administered by the Capacity Building and Funding Management Team. Applications have to be submitted by mid-September.

Small grants are distributed by The Camden Community Chest, which gives £60,000 to about twenty projects that aim to reduce crime and disorder, drug-related activity and anti-social behaviour.

For example, the Fit and Safe project received £1,500 to give free gym passes to young people aged between eleven and nineteen at a local sports centre.

Keeping 'in' with the local authorities

If your application for local government funding is successful you will want to ensure that you maintain the connection you have now made. Most grants run for a year, after which you will need to re-apply if you want yours to continue; so you should ensure that you keep up good relationships with Council Officers, Committee Chairs and your local Ward Councillors.

Remember also that the money you receive is public money for which you will be accountable. The local authority will want to be reassured not only that you are capable of running a good project, but also that your ability to manage money is sound.

The National Lottery

The National Lottery was launched in 1996 and has since raised around £20 billion for good causes. It is run by Camelot under a licence from the Department for Culture Media and Sport and twenty-eight per cent of sales income is handed over to the National Lottery distributors who actually make the grants.

Except for small grants, where application procedures have been simplified, applying for a lottery grant is a major undertaking. You need to design your project (which may include consultation with the community), produce a detailed plan of action and budget, complete a lengthy application form with specific information on levels of benefit and show how you will monitor and evaluate your project. Information on the priorities for each of the distributors, guidelines for applicants and application procedures and forms are on the distributor body's website. To be successful, it is critical that you read this information very carefully and ensure that what you are proposing fits within the criteria of what they want to support.

National Lottery distributors

• Small grants for local communities – Awards for All is a small grants programme aimed at local communities (see page 166).

- Larger grants for community benefit – the Big Lottery Fund receives half the money raised by the lottery for good causes (see below), www.biglottery fund.org.uk.
- Arts grants – the Arts Councils distribute lottery money for the arts (see box on page 167).
- Heritage grants – the Heritage Lottery Fund, www.hlf.org,uk, makes grants to preserve and open up the national heritage. This includes important natural habitats and the countryside, historic parks and gardens, historic buildings and sites, museums and their collections, library collections and archives and the industrial, transport and maritime heritage.
- Film grants are made to stimulate the UK film industry and to promote enjoyment and understanding of cinema. The UK Film Council, www.ukfilmcouncil.org.uk and Scottish Screen, www.scottishscreen.com can all make grants to would-be filmmakers.
- Sports grants are made for excellence in sports, to encourage participation and to improve facilities. The following bodies make grants: Sport England, www.sportengland.org; Sports Council for Wales, www.sports-council-wales.co.uk; Sports Council Northern Ireland, www.sportni.net; SportScotland, www.sportscotland.org.uk; UK Sport (grants to elite sports men and women), www.uksport.gov.uk.

The Big Lottery Fund

The Big Lottery Fund is the main distribution channel for lottery money. It has at its disposal between £600 and £700 million a year (up until 2009 when the arrangements for running the National Lottery will be reviewed). The fund now makes grants within various themed programmes. From time to time, existing programmes close and new ones open, but at the time of writing, these were the main ones:

Must know

Lottery funding

The National Lottery Good Causes Portal has information on how to get Lottery funding, news on the distributor organizations, and case studies of lottery-funded projects: www.lottery goodcauses.org.uk.

• **Reaching communities**. Grants of £10,001 up to £500,000 are made for projects that respond to issues identified in communities and actively involve local people. Priority is given to projects that help those most in need, including people or groups that are hard to reach.

• **Changing Spaces**. This supports community spaces, local community enterprise and access to the natural environment.

• **The Young People's Fund**. Grants are made to individual and groups of young people to help them make a difference in their communities, to voluntary organizations to run local projects for young people and for national projects.

• **The Basis Programme**. Grants of £10,001 up to £500,000 are made to improve support services for voluntary and community organizations.

• **The People's Millions**. Grants are made for larger projects, decided by popular vote and organized in partnership with GMTV and ITV.

• **International grants**. Grants are made to UK-based organizations for overseas development projects.

Awards for All

The Awards for All scheme distributes small grants from the National Lottery. It is organized on a regional basis for England, with similar programmes for Northern Ireland, Scotland and Wales. Grants awarded are from a minimum of £300, up to a maximum of £10,000 for any one organization within a 24-month period.

The application process is really simple. You have to complete a short form and provide a simple budget showing how you propose to spend the money. You must also supply original certified bank statements (as a precaution against fraud).

The aims of Awards for All are to:

• Extend access and participation by encouraging more people to become actively involved in local groups and projects and by supporting activities that aim to be open and accessible to anyone who wishes to take part.

• Increase skill and creativity by supporting activities which help to develop people and organizations, encourage talent and raise standards.

• Improve quality of life by supporting local projects that increase opportunities, provide welfare or environmental benefit or enhance local facilities.

Each region has its own priorities, but these will only become important when the level of applications rises.

Must know

Arts councils

• Arts Council England, www.artscouncil.org.uk
• Arts Council of Northern Ireland www.artscouncil-ni.org
• Arts Council of Wales www.artswales.org.uk
• Scottish Arts Council www.scottisharts.org.uk

Types of projects funded by Awards for All

• A crèche facility for a rural community.
• Publicity materials for a group that recycles computers for community use.
• A programme to involve more disabled people in sport.
• Developing creative writing skills amongst young adults, and enabling their work to be published or performed.
• Organizing a walk featuring buildings of historical interest.
• Sports facilities with qualified coaching for young people on an urban estate.
• A neighbourhood project to promote healthier eating of fruit and vegetables.
• A school wildlife garden.
• Storytelling to introduce people to other cultures.
• Adapting a village hall to improve access for all members of the community.
• A telephone helpline offering advice and support for cancer sufferers and their families.

• Putting on a community play.

For further information on what kinds of charities Awards for All can and cannot fund, visit the website www.awardsforall.org.uk.

European funding

The UK is a member state of the European Union, which makes funds available for the following purposes:

• Promoting the ideals and values of the EU.
• Exchanges between peoples of the EU.
• Addressing poverty and deprivation within the EU.
• Addressing Europe-wide problems and encouraging Europe-wide collaboration for doing so.
• Providing aid to the developing world.

There are two main types of funding from the EU for voluntary organizations. One comes from Structural Funds, management of which has been devolved to member states. The other is from a large number of budget lines for different purposes and these are managed from Brussels by the European Commission.

Structural Funds

The European Regional Development Fund supports the development of backward regions and areas facing structural difficulties. These are known as Objectives 1 and 2. The Department for Communities and Local Government manages this fund and to be eligible for a grant, projects must be located in specified areas.

The European Social Fund supports the development of initiatives in education, training and employment that address issues of unemployment and employability. This is known as Objective 3. The Department for Work and Pensions has responsibility for this budget. Programmes are organized on a regional basis by partnerships led by Government Offices for the Regions and by the government office in Scotland, Wales and Northern Ireland. Partners include local government, higher and further education, the private sector and the voluntary sector. Projects supported need to conform with regional development plans drawn up by the regional partnerships.

Voluntary organizations can apply individually or as members of a consortium (often led by a local authority).

European budget lines

If you are interested in pursuing European budget lines, here are some points to note:
• Many budget lines require a transnational partnership in which applicants are linked up with organizations from at least two other member states.
• Often the project will be co-funded, which means that the balance has to be found from elsewhere. Usually co-funding is 50:50, but in some cases it is 80:20.
• There is a lot of bureaucracy, so you need to be sure you can handle this.
• To access funds requires early information on what's available and possibly a trip to Brussels.

An important feature of European funding is that the money often arrives late, but notwithstanding this the work must be done within the agreed timeframe. This means that an organization may have to find the money up-front to fund its European project.

Want to know more?

• Register to receive information about new Lottery funding programmes by e-mailing: newprogrammes@big lotteryfund.org.uk
• To find out more about grant-making trusts directories go to: www.dsc.org.uk/charitybooks.html
• And visit www.funder finder.org.uk and www.trustfunding.org.uk for a list of trusts that might meet your needs. FunderFinder will tell you where to get their software (tel: 0113 243 3008).
• You can subscribe to a news service on grants to keep you updated on changes in policies and guidelines. Try Charities Information Bureau www.cibfunding.org.uk or Profunding: www.funding information.org.uk
• For info on EU grants see http://europa.eu.int/grants/index_en.htm
• The European Information Service www.lgib.gov.uk publishes *A Guide to European Funding for NGOS*, www.ecas.org.

8 Putting it together

In this chapter, you will find out how to develop a fundraising strategy and an ethical donations policy, which will set the framework for your fundraising. We'll discuss ways of writing a good application (the better your application the better your chances of success), using your time effectively, trustee responsibilities for the money you have raised and the importance of getting going and learning from experience.

Starting out

When you embark on a fundraising project, your first thought is likely to be, 'How can I find the money I need for my project or to cover this year's costs?' In fact, there is another question you should be asking, namely, 'Where will the money be coming from in a few years' time?'

Must know

Multiple sources

Don't become over-dependent on any one source. A large grant can be hard to replace when it ends. Try to boost your independence by having multiple sources of income.

Adopting a fundraising strategy

It is important to think about longer-term solutions to your fundraising as well as how to meet your immediate needs. You may also be asked about your long-term funding plans when you apply for a grant – so it's just as well to have thought this through.

• What might your 'natural sources of income' be? For some organizations these might include membership income, which also demonstrates popular support; some may have partnerships with local authorities, while others might want to remain completely independent of government; some might want a portfolio of foundations to be supporting them as innovators; and others might determine to generate every penny they need through some sort of social enterprise. Work out how you want to be funded. Your job as fundraiser is to make this happen.

• Maximize your assured income and make it grow. Assured income is any income you can rely on from year to year that will not suddenly come to an end.

• Plan well ahead. Try to enter each year with as much of the year's costs already raised or assured. You can then afford to focus more on the longer term.

How dependable are different income sources?

The following are your main sources of income. Those nearest the top are the easiest to acquire and the most dependable; as you move down the list you need to put more effort into the fundraising.

Income from your own resources (where you are in control)
- Income generation from sales of goods and services.
- Income received from rentals, investments and bank interest.

Steady, reliable streams of income
- Annual membership subscriptions.
- Income from standing order donations.
- Income from annual events.
- Long-term contracts and partnerships (which need to be nurtured, and may eventually come to an end).

Actively sought out new income (into which you have put some effort)
- Government grants.
- Trusts and foundations.
- Business support and sponsorship.
   (Most of these provide short- or medium-term income; you need to consider how it will be replaced from the day you receive the first instalment.)

Dreams for the future
- Legacies that start to arrive.
- Major gifts that suddenly appear.
- A successful capital appeal to create an endowment.

Must know

Consistency

Don't go programme hopping. Many organizations raise money by adapting what they do to what funders are prepared to back. Whilst you do need to fit within a funder's criteria, this should not come at the expense of your own aims and objectives.

Do this

Before you start fundraising, you should think about whether there are any sources that you are not prepared to take money from and analyze your reasons for this. If you do decide to have an ethical donations policy, try to link it closely to the work and values of your organization.

The ethics of fundraising

At various points in your fundraising efforts, you may feel challenged from an ethical point of view – uncertain as to whether you should accept money from a particular source because:

• It goes against all that your organization stands for (as in the case of a health charity receiving money from tobacco companies, for example).

• It will compromise your stance; for example, a global warming initiative taking money from an oil major may suggest that it is no longer independent-minded.

• It will lose you support; your young supporters may become really unhappy with your grant from Nestlé, as they may be supporting the baby milk campaign.

On the other hand, you may feel that:

• All money is laundered by the bank – it may go in 'dirty', but comes out clean.

• Working in close partnership with 'the enemy' might give you an opportunity to influence their policies; this was the thinking behind the Shell Better Britain Campaign, which sought to distribute money to local environmental groups – Shell wanted a greener image and sensible dialogue with the environmental movement.

Try not to make decisions for purely political reasons. If you are a charity you have to act in the best interests of your beneficiaries at all times. And it might be in their best interests that you take the money. So, just because Caterpillar vehicles were used to clear settlements in Gaza or BP is doing business in China (where there is concern about the Tibetan people) does not mean that you should turn down donations from either of them. If you feel strongly about these issues, you probably won't want to approach them, but this is different from adopting a policy that formally excludes support from them.

Other ethical issues to consider

• Are you preserving the dignity of your beneficiaries, or portraying them as hopeless and helpless just to raise money?
• Are you telling the truth? It is very easy to distort or overstate the facts to gain support. For example, terrorism kills far fewer people than the motor car, yet we don't have a war on cars.
• Will you do what you promise? (And will this be what people think you have promised?) The tsunami appeal elicited an unprecedented response – people gave because of the immediate need. Yet a year later only one third of the money had been spent, and most affected people were still living in temporary accommodation. Was this what the donors expected?

Writing an application

The sole purpose of your application is to persuade a funder to support you. Although the format for your application varies depending on who you are approaching and for what, the basic formula remains the same:
• Tell them who you are – introduce yourself and your organization.
• State the specific problem or need you plan to address, giving the basic facts. More detailed information can be included in a case study attachment.

Must know

Ethical banking

Some charities select their bank account on ethical grounds; they want to put their money in a bank that actively seeks to do good. Here are some popular options:
• The Co-operative Bank, founded by the co-operative movement, is customer owned and has an ethical focus: www.co-operativebank.co.uk.
• Triodos Bank funds projects of social benefit as its core business: www.triodos.co.uk.
• CafBank is run by the Charities Aid Foundation, which is a charity providing financial services to charities: www.cafbank.co.uk.

Must know

Ethical investing

The issue of socially responsible investment is beyond the scope of this book. Contact the UK Social Investment Forum: www.uksif.org or EIRIS, the ethical investment research service: www.eiris.org.

• Say what you are proposing to do and how. If you are writing a long application, start with a couple of sentences summarizing your project before moving on to the details. Set measurable outputs and outcomes.

• A catchy project title is also helpful – 'Changing Playgrounds' is better than 'The Hackney School Playground Improvement Project'.

• Say how much you are looking for, and how much you would like them to give. You can provide an overall sum or just figures for the main expenditure heads. A more detailed budget can be attached.

• Suggest to them why they might want to fund it – is it a project that reflects their interests or policies, for example? You might also want to mention how the project might be funded in the long term – they are unlikely to want to fund something that has no future.

• Conclude by saying that you are happy to send them more information or answer any questions, and invite them to visit you to see your work and to meet some of the people you are working with.

Before you apply

Before you write your application check the following:

• Is there an official application form? If so, you must use it.

• Has the funder produced written guidelines for applicants. If so, read them very carefully, ensuring that what you are proposing fits in with what they want to fund (in terms of their priorities as well as their policies).

• Is there a prescribed length for applications? You don't want to produce a ten-page masterpiece, only to find that applications of more than four pages will not be considered.

• Do you have the full name and job title of the person you are writing to and are they correctly spelled? It is worth making a phone call to check this.

• Is there a deadline for applications? Many government funds are distributed annually and if you miss the deadline, you will have to wait until the following year. Trusts often consider applications quarterly, which makes timing less of an issue.

You are not being paid for the words you write, but to meet a need or address a problem. Demonstrate the need and what you are going to do about it as effectively as you can:

• Your first paragraph or what you say in a covering letter must grab the reader's attention – make them sit up and want to read on.

• Make your application as concise as possible. While major sponsorship proposals or applications to government bodies or the National Lottery call for a lot of information, most trusts and companies require no more than a couple of pages.

• Try to inject something of your own personality. As one fundraiser said: 'I always start off by telling them that I can't read or write ... and the funny thing is that I'm often successful!'

• Refer to any meetings or conversations you have had with the person you are writing to; it always helps if you are known to them.

How applications are processed

An application may or may not be acknowledged upon receipt – many funders receive hundreds of applications a month. A quick scan will tell them

Must know

Three golden rules

1. **You cannot tell them everything. There isn't the space ... and they wouldn't read it all anyway.**
2. **Ask them to support something specific that is of interest to them, rather than just make a grant to your organization.**
3. **Show examples of real people, what their problems are, and how your work is helping them.**

Must know

Application advice

• **Make your application as personal as possible – anything resembling a circular will end up in the bin.**
• **Ensure that your application is neat, tidy and error-free – proofread it for typos and see that the budget adds up.**
• **Include the name and contact details of someone who can be called to discuss the application further and ensure that person is properly briefed.**

whether or not the proposal fits within their guidelines. Surprisingly, a large number do not and these will be rejected at this stage.

The application will then be assessed, either by a member of staff, a trustee or a paid consultant. (Some larger trusts devolve decisions on smaller grants to staff and some large companies allow local managers to make decisions on small grants.) This process might involve a meeting, telephone discussion or project visit, although many applications are assessed only on the basis of the information sent in. A recommendation is then made to the Grants Committee.

The Grants Committee will meet and make a decision. Sometimes the Committee will approve all recommendations made, at other times the decision as to which cause to support will reflect available funds. The applicant will then be informed as to the outcome.

In the case of a rejection, the applicant may be given a reason but this is not always the case. In the case of a successful application, the funder may make a grant subject to certain conditions as set out in a letter of acceptance to be signed by the applicant.

The grant is usually paid in advance and in either one or several instalments.

How to write a better application
You can always write a better application. You are not looking for perfection, but for something that will do a good job in helping you raise money. Here's a suggested process for achieving this:
• Don't be vague. Support your appeal with facts and figures wherever possible.

- Give examples or short case studies to illustrate some of your points.
- Stress your credibility. Don't be shy about how good you are and what you have been able to achieve.
- Endorsements really do work. Get someone who is important and respected to write a covering letter praising your achievements. This will have an impact on the person reading your application.

Editing what you have written

If your application is well written and the information 'jumps from the page', it is more likely to go onto the 'Action' pile than the 'Reject' pile. In order to achieve this, you need to edit your work carefully. This means ensuring that the content is well organized and the information is correct, making sure that it is readable and that you proofread what you have written. To make what you have written more readable:

- Use a red pencil to edit what you have written.
- Try cutting it by a quarter – it will almost certainly improve as a result.
- Insert headlines and sub-heads as signposts for the reader.
- Insert frequent paragraph breaks to shorten the paragraphs; large blocks of text can be hard to read.
- Turn continuous prose into lists and bullet points; this will highlight the points you want to make.
- Turn a complex sentence into two or more shorter, simpler ones.
- Clarify a difficult point by adding a bit more explanation.
- Spell out acronyms (at least the first time they appear in the text).

Must know

Read the small print

If your application is successful, you may be asked to sign a form stating that you agree to the terms and conditions of the grant. Read through this carefully and if there is anything that bothers you or which you don't understand, contact the funder to discuss it. Only sign once you have understood and agreed everything.

Exercises

Use simpler words. For each of the following words, suggest a more concise alternative:

• despite the fact that..

• an abundance of...

• in the majority of cases.......................................

• close proximity to..

• in the event that ....

• utilization...

Use simpler sentences. Try finding a more succinct way to say the following:

• It is our belief that there should be consultation by the administrators with the delivery staff before any changes in the regulations are made.

• The international proliferation of drugs – more than 10,000 prescription and over 100,000 non-prescription drugs – instead of being a boon has created major problems for developing countries which are unable to regulate their quality, sale or distribution.

• The implementation of participatory evaluation methodologies amongst the target communities should be deferred one year in order for field staff to enhance their understanding of the techniques that will be used.

• Use shorter and easily understood words rather than longer words and jargon – you want the reader to understand what you are saying.

• Write in the first person and use active rather than passive verbs. Saying 'We are organizing a training course' is more effective than 'Training courses are being organized'.

Saying thank you and reporting back

The first donation that you receive may be the first of many, but this depends largely on you. If you take the money and do nothing more, you will be damaging your chances of further support. Saying thank you, reporting back and nurturing a good relationship with your donors by keeping in touch are extremely important.

• Send an e-mail immediately the grant is confirmed and a formal letter when the donation arrives. If someone has helped you to ask for the money, send them a letter of thanks as well.

• Think about thanking them less formally, too. A telephone call or a handwritten letter would convey to them that you really are thrilled. There is often a difficulty if you have been expecting a £5,000 donation and only £500 arrives. Do you refer to this as a generous donation? Do you query the amount? You have to decide what to do. But thank them none the less, as their support will help you to carry out your work.

• Next time you meet them, make a point of telling them about your progress.

Reporting back

• The terms and conditions of the grant will almost certainly require that you report back and state a timetable for doing this. You will almost certainly have to submit an annual project report and your organization's annual accounts. Put a note in your diary about three weeks before the due date, so as to make sure you have enough time to get all the information together.

• Keep them posted regarding your progress. If there are unexpected successes or snags, let them know. If there is newspaper coverage, send them a photocopy. They are an investor in your work, and they will be interested to hear how you are doing.

Keeping in touch

• At some time during the year, consider holding a meeting or presentation for your donors to update them and to meet some of your beneficiaries. A celebrity host for this event would make it a great draw (see page 113).

• Invite them to any event you may be holding as part of the programme of work that they have been supporting.

• Put them on your database to receive regular updates or newsletters. But take care not to bombard them with so much information that they begin to feel harassed.

• If you want some advice or their reaction to an idea you are developing, or when something terrific has happened, why not telephone them? If they seem really interested, you could think about inviting them to lunch or for a coffee to talk through some of your ideas.

• Send them a Christmas card with a short handwritten note wishing them all the best for the coming year.

Using your time effectively

You have limited time and resources to spend on your fundraising, so make sure you use these well by planning ahead and making cost-effective use of your time.

It can take several months to plan a major grant application, more to prepare and discuss it with the funder, then up to six months for it to go through the decision process. Similarly, it can take the best part of a year to plan a fundraising event; so start on next year's as soon as this year's is finished.

Aim to start each year with the assurance that most of the money you need has already been raised (or is in the process of being raised), which will make the fundraising job more manageable.

Make sure that you are spending your time on those things that (a) are more likely to lead to a positive outcome and (b) generate more income for you. You will be surprised at how much of your time has to be spent on basic administration, internal meetings and answering e-mails. This makes it doubly important to use your time effectively.

Try to balance the following factors when deciding how to allocate your time:
• The time and effort involved.
• The skills and resources needed (and whether you have or can get them).
• The expected sum that will be raised (and whether your efforts this year will result in money being raised in subsequent years).
• The chances of success (and the risk of failure).

It is probably worthwhile spending more time on building relationships and less time on asking; more time on a few carefully selected fundraising initiatives and less on a scattergun approach; more time on an application for a big grant that stands a high chance of success, and less on organizing an event that will raise very little.

Get help where necessary

You may need to find other people to help you, either because you just don't have the time available, or because you need to bring in extra skills.

Using volunteers can be ideal if you find someone who is just right. While a volunteer doesn't come free – they will have expenses and they will require support – this is still a low-cost option if they deliver on what they promise.

Fundraising consultants are another option. This can be costly, so make sure you find the right person (take references from previous clients) and use them effectively. Paying them a percentage of what they raise lessens your risk but creates an ethical problem. The 1992 Charities Act requires you to enter into a contract with the professional fundraiser and that they declare to donors the basis on which they are being remunerated. This may make the donor less inclined to give,

Must know

Time planning

To maximize what you achieve in the time available give priority to:
• Fundraising opportunities with a high chance of success.
• Opportunities with the potential to raise a lot of money.
• Fundraising that generates money not just for this year, but creates a stream of income for future years.

however. Alternatively, you could employ either a full- or part-time fundraising assistant or someone to provide administrative support.

Trustee responsibilities

One of the main trustee responsibilities with regard to fundraising is to ensure that if money is given for a specified purpose, the charity uses it for that purpose. If it is spent on something else, the trustees will be 'in breach of trust'. This could lead to a prison sentence in the event of fraud or in trustees having to repay the misspent money out of their own pockets if it happened unwittingly.

If the money can't be spent for the specified purposes, the charity has to go back to the donor and ask for permission to spend it in another way. If this isn't given, the money must be returned.

It was for this reason that Médécins Sans Frontières halted its tsunami appeal once it realized that it had raised more than enough. For public appeals, many charities attach a rider (often in small print) stating that they retain discretion to spend the money on other purposes, or alternatively they choose wording that does not imply a binding commitment to spend the money in a particular way: '£10 would plant a rose bush...' rather than '£10 will plant a rose bush...'.

Ensuring that the donor's conditions are met is another important trustee responsibility so they must instigate procedures to ensure it is done. This is particularly relevant for large grants from public bodies where there may be a whole range of conditions regarding public accountability, keeping of accounts, supplying reports and evaluation.

Trustee liability

If a charity is incurring all sorts of actual, contingent and potential liabilities (such as putting a building into good repair at the end of a lease, or employee liability for redundancy payments if it ceases to operate), it is best that the charity be constituted or re-constituted with limited liability, so that these are no longer the trustees' personal liabilities. There is also the option of taking out Trustee Liability Insurance. However, most insurance policies will not cover wilful breach of trust and trustees are not really at risk if they act in good faith. Trustees should decide collectively whether or not they need to be insured.

Other trustee responsibilities

In addition to the two main responsibilities described above, the trustees must also ensure that the charity:
• Operates within its charitable purposes and beneficial area (as set out in its constitution).
• Meets the Charities Act requirements for fundraising; this includes conditions on employing professional fundraisers and for collecting money from the public.
• Has the resources to meet its liabilities and is not trading insolvently.
• Uses its resources cost effectively and for maximum impact.
• Prepares annual accounts and files them with the appropriate regulatory bodies (for a charitable

Do this

Understand your trustee responsibilities in relation to the money you raise and make sure that these are met.

Think about this

Fundraising is about getting the resources to make people's dreams for a better world come true. It is an important way of helping to make your local community and the world a better place.

company in England, this would be the Charity Commission and Companies House).

• Always acts in the best interests of the beneficiaries.

• Operates within the law – for example, regarding health and safety, employer responsibilities and child protection.

• Sets in place any ethical policy regarding investments, bank accounts and receipt of donations – subject to acting in the best interests of the beneficiaries.

A call to action!

Now you know all you need to know about fundraising and it's time to put the theory into practice. The best learning will come from your own experience, so start raising money, then learn to do it better and better! Just to recap:

• Decide what you need to raise money for.

• Calculate how much you need.

• Think about who you might ask and how much they might give.

• Present a case for why they should support you that will inspire them to do so.

• Then go out and ask, using all the ideas and advice in this book.

Remember that you won't succeed every time, but be prepared to learn from failures and disappointment. Accept that not everyone is willing to give, and recognize that you may have a string of failures before you achieve a single success.

Be persistent. Be optimistic. Be cheerful. Be enthusiastic. Be inspiring. Be yourself!

And remember that if you don't ask, you won't get, which means that a disadvantaged or needy person will continue to suffer, a much-needed facility won't be built or a problem that affects the whole community will not be addressed.

So go for it. Do it as well as you can. And the best of luck!

Want to know more?

• On pages 188-9 you will find a list of organizations and publications that can provide further advice and support for your fundraising efforts.

• See chapter 7 for information on applying for grants. In particular, remember that the Awards for All scheme (see pagea 166-8) should be considered a 'must apply' for many charities.

Need to know more?

Throughout this book, there are sources of information relating to particular aspects of fundraising (such as getting funding from Europe or keeping up-to-date on trust funding). In this section you will find a list of general resources.

Organizations and websites

Charities Aid Foundation is a charity providing financial services to charities and to charity donors, including banking, direct debit management, payroll giving, loans and grants, planned giving: www.cafonline.org.

Charity Commission registers and regulates charities in England and Wales, maintains a Register of Charities and publishes information to enable charities and charity trustees to operate more effectively. The Register of Charities contains annual reports and accounts and it may be worth looking at charities whose work is similar to yours: www.charity-commission.gov.uk.

Community Matters is the National Federation of Community Organizations, targeting organizations that are smaller and more local than the NCVO membership: www.community matters.org.uk.

Directory of Social Change publishes and distributes grant guides and

fundraising handbooks. They also run basic fundraising training. Contact them for their catalogue and training programme, and ask to be put on their (free) e-mailing list: www.dsc.org.uk.

Giving Nation, now operated under the wing of the Citizenship Foundation, this encourages charitable giving by young people: www.g-nation.co.uk.

Guidestar is a database on every charity in the UK: www.guidestar.org.uk.

Institute of Fundraising is the professional body in the UK that supports and represents fundraisers and the fundraising profession. This will be mainly of interest to fundraisers working for larger and medium-sized charities: www.institute-of-fundraising.org.uk.

Justgiving helps charities to reclaim tax and provides web pages for participants in sponsored fundraising events to help them raise money: www.justgiving.com.

National Council of Voluntary Organizations is the representative body for the voluntary sector in England, and has the AskNCVO information service: www.ncvo-vol.org.uk. See also: Scottish Council for Voluntary Organizations: www.scvo.org.uk; Wales Council for Voluntary Action: www.wcva.org.uk; Northern Ireland

Council for Voluntary Action: www.nicva.org.

New Philanthropy Capital analyzes charities on behalf of donors and suggests ways of improving effectiveness: www.philanthropy capital.org.

Resource Alliance, formerly known as the International Fund Raising Workshop, helps voluntary organizations worldwide to build their fundraising capacity by organizing conferences and workshops: www.resource-alliance.org.

The UK Social Investment Forum is a network for financial and philanthropic institutions interested in social investing and loan-making: www.uksif.org.

Books and other information sources
Directory of Social Change has the best range of publications, including its own titles, the Charities Aid Foundation's publications and some selected books that are included on its list. Get on the DSC mailing list to receive information on publications: www.dsc.org.uk/charity books.html.

Amazon Type 'Fundraising' into www. amazon.co.uk and a list of nearly 400 different titles will appear. The top eight sellers are:
Event Planning: the Ultimate Guide to Successful Meetings...Fundraising Galas, by Judy Allen

The Complete Fundraising Handbook, by Nina Botting and Michael Norton
How to Write Successful Fundraising Letters, by Mal Warwick
Writing Better Fundraising Applications, by Michael Eastwood and Michael Norton
Relationship Fundraising, by Ken Burnett
The Complete Guide to Fundraising, by P F and P W Sterrett
Tried and Tested Ideas for Local Fundraising, by Sarah Passingham
Fundraising Management: Analysis, Planning and Practice, by Adrian Sargeant and Elaine Jay

Resource Alliance publishes the *WorldWide Fundraisers' Handbook*, aimed at NGOs around the world.

Charities Information Bureau provides e-mail information through its *CIBfunding Newsletter*. This is a must for anyone wanting to keep up to date on the latest funding opportunities: www.cibfunding.org.uk.

Smart Resources is a news service for charities, faith-based organizations and social enterprises: www.smartresources.org.

Third Sector is a professional magazine for those working in charities: www.thirdsector.co.uk.

Index

Index